Rona Munro

JAMES IV: QUEEN OF THE FIGHT

NICK HERN BOOKS
London
www.nickhernbooks.co.uk

A Nick Hern Book

James IV: Queen of the Fight first published in Great Britain as a paperback original in 2022 by Nick Hern Books Limited, The Glasshouse, 49a Goldhawk Road, London W12 8QP

Cover artwork: design by Niall Walker; photograph of actors Laura Lovemore, Danielle Jam and Danielle Cahill by Mihaela Bodlovic

Designed and typeset by Nick Hern Books, London
Printed in Great Britain by Mimeo Ltd, Huntingdon, Cambridgeshire PE29 6XX

A CIP catalogue record for this book is available from the British Library

ISBN 978 1 83904 1 327

RONA MUNRO

Rona Munro has written extensively for stage, radio, film and television including the recent adaptations of *My Name Is Lucy Barton* for the Bridge Theatre, London and Manhattan Theatre Company on Broadway, New York, and *Captain Corelli's Mandolin* for Neil Laidlaw Productions. She wrote the award-winning trilogy *The James Plays* for the National Theatre of Scotland, the National Theatre of Great Britain and the Edinburgh International Festival. This is the fourth play in that series about the medieval history of Scotland. *Mary*, a production for Hampstead Theatre in London, is the sixth.

Other credits include award-winning plays *Iron* for the Traverse Theatre and Royal Court London, *The Maiden Stone* for Hampstead Theatre, *Little Eagles* and *The Indian Boy* for the Royal Shakespeare Company, and *Bold Girls* for 7:84 Theatre Scotland.

Film and TV work includes *Oranges and Sunshine*, directed by Jim Loach and starring Emily Watson and Hugo Weaving, the Ken Loach film *Ladybird, Ladybird*, which won a Silver Bear at the Berlin Festival, *Aimée & Jaguar*, a Silver Bear winner and Golden Globe nomination, and BAFTA nominated *Bumping the Odds* for the BBC. She has also written many other single plays for TV and contributed to series such as *Doctor Who*.

Other Titles in this Series

Mike Bartlett
THE 47TH
ALBION
BULL
GAME
AN INTERVENTION
KING CHARLES III
MIKE BARTLETT PLAYS: TWO
MRS DELGADO
SCANDALTOWN
SNOWFLAKE
VASSA *after* Gorky
WILD

Jez Butterworth
THE FERRYMAN
JERUSALEM
JEZ BUTTERWORTH PLAYS: ONE
JEZ BUTTERWORTH PLAYS: TWO
MOJO
THE NIGHT HERON
PARLOUR SONG
THE RIVER
THE WINTERLING

Caryl Churchill
BLUE HEART
CHURCHILL PLAYS: THREE
CHURCHILL PLAYS: FOUR
CHURCHILL PLAYS: FIVE
CHURCHILL: SHORTS
CLOUD NINE
DING DONG THE WICKED
A DREAM PLAY *after* Strindberg
DRUNK ENOUGH TO SAY I LOVE YOU?
ESCAPED ALONE
FAR AWAY
GLASS. KILL. BLUEBEARD'S FRIENDS. IMP.
HERE WE GO
HOTEL
ICECREAM
LIGHT SHINING IN BUCKINGHAMSHIRE
LOVE AND INFORMATION
MAD FOREST
A NUMBER
PIGS AND DOGS
SEVEN JEWISH CHILDREN
THE SKRIKER
THIS IS A CHAIR
THYESTES *after* Seneca
TRAPS
WHAT IF IF ONLY

Natasha Gordon
NINE NIGHT

Lucy Kirkwood
BEAUTY AND THE BEAST *with* Katie Mitchell
BLOODY WIMMIN
THE CHILDREN
CHIMERICA
HEDDA *after* Ibsen
IT FELT EMPTY WHEN THE HEART WENT AT FIRST BUT IT IS ALRIGHT NOW
LUCY KIRKWOOD PLAYS: ONE
MOSQUITOES
NSFW
RAPTURE
TINDERBOX
THE WELKIN

Liz Lochhead
BLOOD AND ICE
DRACULA *after* Stoker
EDUCATING AGNES ('The School for Wives') *after* Molière
GOOD THINGS
LIZ LOCHHEAD: FIVE PLAYS
MARY QUEEN OF SCOTS GOT HER HEAD CHOPPED OFF
MEDEA *after* Euripides
MISERYGUTS ('The Miser') & TARTUFFE *after* Molière
PERFECT DAYS
THEBANS *after* Euripides & Sophocles
THON MAN MOLIÈRE

Linda McLean
ANY GIVEN DAY
GLORY ON EARTH
ONE GOOD BEATING
RIDDANCE
SEX & GOD
SHIMMER
STRANGERS, BABIES

Rona Munro
THE ASTRONAUT'S CHAIR
BOLD GIRLS
CAPTAIN CORELLI'S MANDOLIN *after* Louis de Bernières
THE HOUSE OF BERNARDA ALBA *after* Lorca
THE INDIAN BOY
IRON
THE JAMES PLAYS
THE LAST WITCH
LITTLE EAGLES
LONG TIME DEAD
THE MAIDEN STONE
MARY
MARY BARTON *after* Gaskell
MARY SHELLEY'S FRANKENSTEIN *after* Mary Shelley
PANDAS
SCUTTLERS
STRAWBERRIES IN JANUARY *from* de la Chenelière
YOUR TURN TO CLEAN THE STAIR & FUGUE

Stef Smith
ENOUGH
GIRL IN THE MACHINE
HUMAN ANIMALS
NORA : A DOLL'S HOUSE
REMOTE
SWALLOW

debbie tucker green
BORN BAD
DEBBIE TUCKER GREEN PLAYS: ONE
DIRTY BUTTERFLY
EAR FOR EYE
HANG
NUT
A PROFOUNDLY AFFECTIONATE, PASSIONATE DEVOTION TO SOMEONE (– *NOUN*)
RANDOM
STONING MARY
TRADE & GENERATIONS
TRUTH AND RECONCILIATION

James IV: Queen of the Fight was first produced by Raw Material and Capital Theatres in association with National Theatre of Scotland and first performed at the Festival Theatre, Edinburgh, on 30 September 2022, before touring. The cast was as follows:

TURNBULL/ENSEMBLE	Ewan Black
JAMES IV	Daniel Cahill
DONALD	Malcolm Cumming
DAME PHEMY	Blythe Duff
DUNBAR	Keith Fleming
MARGARET	Sarita Gabony
ELLEN	Danielle Jam
ANNE	Laura Lovemore
PETER	Thierry Mabonga
DOUGLAS/ENSEMBLE	Samuel Pashby
ENSEMBLE/ MUSICAL SUPERVISOR	Gameli Tordzro

Writer/Executive Producer	Rona Munro
Director/Executive Producer	Laurie Sansom
Designer	Jon Bausor
Movement Director	Neil Bettles
Composer	Paul Leonard-Morgan
Lighting Designer	Lizzie Powell
Sound Designer	Garry Boyle
Fight Directors	Rachel Bown-Williams & Ruth Cooper-Brown of RC-Annie
Historical Consultant	Dr Onyeka Nubia
Associate Director (Rehearsals)	Jaïrus Obayomi
Associate Director (Tour)	Luke Kernaghan
Casting Director	Laura Donnelly CDG
Executive Producer	Margaret-Anne O'Donnell
Executive Producer	Gillian Garrity

Raw Material

With over twenty years' independent experience making and touring celebrated Scottish theatre around the world, Margaret-Anne O'Donnell and Gillian Garrity, founded Raw Material, an award-winning, independent producing house based in Scotland in 2018,

We believe theatre plays a crucial role in championing socio-political change. Our shared ambition to develop, create and tour bold accessible theatre that inspires, entertains and captivates audiences across borders formed the foundations of our company. We are advocates for access and diversity within the theatre sector and are passionate about enabling creative ambition, developing new models for success and supporting all stages of making theatre happen. We celebrate and applaud the artists, creatives, production teams, marketeers, funders, partners and audiences who continue to support the creation and touring of Scottish theatre both at home and abroad.

To find out more about our work or to support us further **www.rawmaterialarts.com** or find us on social media @RAWMaterialArts

Since inception in 2018, Raw Material has produced work both in the UK and internationally. Productions include *James IV: Queen of the Fight* by Rona Munro (Raw Material & Capital Theatres in association with National Theatre of Scotland, UK 2022), *The Stamping Ground* by Morna Young (Raw Material & Eden Court Highlands, UK 2022 & 2023), *In The Interest of Safety Can Patrons Kindly Supervise Their Children at all Times* (21Common & Raw Material, UK 2022, supported by Made In Scotland), *Unicorn Christmas Party* by Sarah Rose Graber & Ruxy Cantir (Raw Material, HMT Aberdeen, Eden Court Highlands & Capital Theatres, Scotland 2021, 2022 & 2023), *Unicorn Dance Party* by Sarah Rose Graber & Ruxy Cantir (Raw Material, Scotland 21 & 22), *The Signalman* by Peter Arnott (Raw Material & Perth Theatre, UK 2021), *Glasgow Girls* by David Grieg & Cora Bissett (Raw Material in association with Regular Music, UK & international 2019), *Dancing in the Streets* by Janice Parker (Raw Material, Edinburgh International Festival, UK 2019), *What Girls Are*

Made Of by Cora Bissett (Raw Material & Traverse Theatre, UK & international 2018 & 2019, supported by Made In Scotland), *We Are In Time* by Untitled Projects & Scottish Ensemble (produced by Raw Material, UK 2019), *After The Cuts* by Gary McNair (Raw Material & Beacon Arts Centre, UK 2018), *Off Kilter* by Ramesh Meyyappan (Raw Material, Tron Theatre & TheatreWorks, Singapore, UK & international 2018/19), *The Spinners* by Limosani Projeks & Al Seed (Raw Material, UK 2019).

Capital Theatres

Capital Theatres present world-class shows to entertain and inspire audiences of all ages.

In a normal year we stage over 700 performances, at the Festival Theatre (1,900 seats), the King's Theatre (1,300 seats) and The Studio (155 seats), in a broad and inclusive programme featuring the very best in drama, dance, musical theatre, live music, comedy and pantomime.

In June 2021 we reopened the doors to our buildings and welcomed audiences back for the first time since the pandemic turned our theatres dark. Since then we have announced a series of co-productions including *James IV: Queen of the Fight*, *Sunshine on Leith* and three festive early-years commissions, the first of which, *The Enormous Christmas Turnip*, premiered in The Studio in December 2021 while the second, *The Gift*, will play there this Christmas. We've also progressed our talent development strand through our Musical Commissioning Hub.

Much of our programme is exclusive to our venues in Scotland, providing the only opportunity for audiences to see the biggest shows touring north of the border, the best in international contemporary dance and the latest productions from leading local and national companies.

We support access to the arts for everyone and have an extensive creative engagement programme of talks, workshops and events to introduce and develop engagement and interest in the heritage of our buildings and all areas of live performance.

This year we plan to begin the capital redevelopment of the King's to turn it into both a thriving community hub and a world-class venue while maintaining its history and heritage. You can learn more about how to support this transformational redevelopment by visiting our website.

We are a registered Scottish charity (SC018605) and our theatres and our programme are supported by the City of Edinburgh Council.

www.capitaltheatres.com

The National Theatre of Scotland

The National Theatre of Scotland is dedicated to playing the great stages, arts centres, village halls, schools and site-specific locations of Scotland, the UK and internationally. As well as creating groundbreaking productions and working with the most talented theatre-makers, the National Theatre of Scotland produces significant community engagement projects, innovates digitally and works constantly to develop new talent. Central to this is finding pioneering ways to reach current and new audiences and to encourage people's full participation in the Company's work. With no performance building of its own, the Company works with existing and new venues and companies to create and tour theatre of the highest quality. Founded in 2006, the Company, in its short life, has become a globally significant theatrical player, with an extensive repertoire of award-winning work. The National Theatre of Scotland is supported by the Scottish Government.

www.nationaltheatrescotland.com

Author's Note

Rona Munro

The *Queen of the Fight* is a stand-alone story but it's also the fourth play in a series that began with *The James Plays* trilogy, first staged in 2014. My desire to write a history cycle focusing on the medieval kings and queens of Scotland arose when I first saw the Royal Shakespeare Company stage the entire cycle of Shakespeare's history plays over three days. That was an extraordinary theatrical experience. Watching it I realised two things: we had no equivalent theatrical celebration of Scottish history, and almost all popular accessible understanding of that period of English history came first from those plays. Every time I have a conversation with anyone about *The James Plays*, they invariably say the same thing, 'I don't know anything about this history.' Hardly anyone does, but possibly no one in the general population would know about Henry V or Richard III without Shakespeare. I've no illusions I can match Shakespeare but I thought someone should try and dramatise Scotland's history. History is the foundation that forms our present, I think popular culture can do a really important job, examining and revealing the nature of the ground on which we now stand.

Other plays in this series have been completed and some are moving into production as I'm writing this. However each play stands alone, an audience doesn't need to have seen the previous instalments, but there are Easter eggs and rewards for those who have.

The obstacles to making this particular invisible history visible were, for me, quite daunting. The events of the *Queen of the Fight* are based on historical facts but they challenge most people's perception of the true diversity of Scottish history and how long ago it was that people from a wider world were first absorbed into the community of Scotland. I was certainly labouring under several misconceptions. I gradually discovered these to be inaccurate as I finally located the work of historians who have made a detailed study of original source material about Black British history. The insights that allowed mystifying historical events to become explicable came most particularly from Dr Onyeka Nubia when he became our historical consultant for the first production.

The starting point for my research for the play itself was a poem written by the fifteenth-century Scottish makar William Dunbar. This one is usually called 'Ane Blak Moor' (A Black Moor). It describes a woman who was the centre of royal tournaments, the 'Queen of the Fight'. It's one of the first references to anyone from the global majority in Scottish literature, and it is very clearly derogatory and demeaning. It has been written to hurt someone, to diminish them.

As a first literary milestone for Scotland it does us no favours. But what both troubled and fascinated me was that I felt William Dunbar was a gifted writer. His poetry is, in my uneducated opinion, a mixed bag, some of the poems seem like elaborate imitations of famous medieval English writers but many others, especially those written unequivocally in Scots, are startling in their immediacy. Once you have the tools to penetrate the more archaic language you are reading vivid descriptions of such mundane torments as headaches, poignant evocations of the fear of death, human experiences and emotions that are the same as they ever were. He also returns over and over to another theme that speaks particularly to any writer's experience, the struggle of the freelancer trying to get a wage for their work from an erratic group of patrons.

As a Scottish writer, looking back at another across a gap of centuries, I felt, possibly in my arrogance, that I might be particularly well equipped to try and understand how that particular poem, 'Ane Blak More', came to be written. That was the starting point of this story and I hope the play suggests some possible answers – fiction, speculation, but answers that make sense to me. Dunbar has his legacy and his published record. If I am slandering a ghost I hope at least we are making others who were part of his story visible as they have not been before.

If you are reading this script with a view to staging it I’ll say what I say to every director: the staging suggestions and stage directions are simply that, suggestions, to be used only if helpful. But please don’t mess around with the words. There should be a good reason for every line.

September 2022

Characters

ELLEN, *from African Moorish Iberia, early twenties*
ANNE, *from African Moorish Iberia, mid-twenties*
PETER, *from African Moorish Iberia, early thirties*
JAMES, *King of Scots, thirty-four*
DUNBAR, *Scottish makar (poet), forty-seven*
MARGARET, *English, Queen of Scots, seventeen*
DAME PHEMY
DONALD, *Gael, heir to Lordship of Isles, seventeen*
TURNBULL, *Scottish farmer/laird, twenties*
ARCHIBALD DOUGLAS, *Scottish aristocrat, twenties*
FARMER, *Scottish aristocrat, twenties*

And FIGHTERS, MUSICIANS

All poetry by William Dunbar

This text went to press before the end of rehearsals and so may differ slightly from the play as performed.

ACT ONE

ELLEN. When oor story's over and done, oor names micht be forgotten. But we were real. The King was real, his Queen was real, the songs were sung and heard and all the dances had their steps. The deid were living as we live now.

The poem was real jist as the makar made it.

Remember? Can you mind who we were?

On the Canongate, Edinburgh

ELLEN *moves to stand close to* ANNE. *They're part of a group of travellers, newly arrived at Holyrood, looking round at a cold, strange world. They're dazed and wary. After a moment* ANNE *starts singing softly – 'Tres Morillas', a traditional song.*

ELLEN *is too tense to join in.*

ANNE. *Todo va a ir bien.* [It will be alright.]

ELLEN *nods.* ANNE *sings again,* ELLEN *joins in.*

As the song finishes they hold each other a moment.

ELLEN. *Nosotras estaremos bien.* [*We're going to be alright.*]

They still hold onto each other as they're aware of more people are arriving, a crowd, it's alarming. They're crowding round the gate of Holyrood to see the new arrivals and the King. Then PETER *is on, announcing* JAMES *and* MARGARET.

PETER. King James! Give honour to James and his richt bonny Queen!

PETER *leads applause and cheering as* JAMES *and* MARGARET *process out. In all crowd scenes, if there's time and space,* JAMES *is greeting and acknowledging ordinary people in the crowd. He is hand in hand with* MARGARET.

JAMES (*indicating the travellers*). Scotland now we have the *best* the world has to offer right enough. Will you look at this? These travellers are royal attendants and entertainers from Europe, from Moorish Spain. They were travelling to serve at the court of Henry Seventh of England, but eh… well they were diverted, shall we say. Aye, the English and Portuguese have robbed enough Scottish shipping, nae harm we help oursels to a wee bit of theirs eh?

So these folk have had a rough welcome, we need tae gie them better noo.

(*To the travellers.*) *¡Bienvenidos a Escocia!*

This is a place of peace.

(*To crowd.*) Am I right?

Aye, you'll see, all the world is welcome here, you're safe behind our strong walls. This land is defended by the bravest fighters and nae enemy daur cam near oor border.

You'll find braw folk and guid meat and drink and song and dance and spectacle. I'll promise mair. You'll find love. The love o' good neighbours, the love that keeps God's peace and maks it sweeter. Like the love atween me and my bonny English bride.

He pulls MARGARET *to face him. They gaze into each other's eyes adoringly. They kiss.*

The crowd goes nuts.

Then MARGARET *is leaving, smiling and acknowledging the crowd as they cheer.*

(*To* PETER.) Bring the travellers into the palace! Find places for them all.

JAMES *is off.* PETER *is bringing the travellers through the gate of Holyrood Palace, Edinburgh.*

PETER. Back, you gypet gawpies! Let the travellers through.

The scene transforms to –

Courtyard

The travellers are being brought in. DUNBAR *slips in with them, trying to get* PETER*'s attention.*

DUNBAR. My lord! Lord Peter! It's me! Dunbar, remember? Dunbar the makar. What a day eh? You'll be needing a few words tae celebrate a day like this!

PETER. Not today, Dunbar.

(*Calling out.*) Close the gate, close the gate.

DAME PHEMY *is on, hurrying through the courtyard.*

DAME PHEMY. They're here already! Why was I no called?

DUNBAR *is trying to intercept her.*

DUNBAR. My lady, are you needing any letters… a wee flyting written mebbe…?

DAME PHEMY. Who let you in, Dunbar? Oot my way.

She checks as she sees PETER *is lining the travellers up and addressing them.*

PETER. *Necesitamos sirvientes de la corte. Necesitamos Músicos.* Any musicians?

DAME PHEMY. What do you think you're daein?

PETER *turns to her.*

PETER. The King asked me to find places for the travellers…

DAME PHEMY (*cuts in on him*). The King asked you to find servants for his household? For the Queen's household? That's your job an a' noo, is it?

PETER. No, I jist…

DAME PHEMY (*cutting in*). Because last time I checked *we* were the keepers of the royal household. Me and my lord, has the King told you different?

PETER. I'm finding musicians.

DAME PHEMY. Aye. Good. On you go. Organise the entertainment and keep your neb oot o' my business.

She turns to ANNE *and* ELLEN.

Right. Straighten up, lassies, een o' you's aboot tae get lucky. The Queen hersel wants a Moorish attendant. I'm telt there's royal attendants here. Is that you?

ANNE *does not appreciate this tone. She moves a little protectively in front of* ELLEN, *glaring at* DAME PHEMY.

ANNE. *¿Por qué grita esa mujer?* [Why is this woman shouting?]

Behind this PETER *has identified a* MUSICIAN/ MUSICIANS. *Talking quietly in Spanish, he's negotiating with them.*

ELLEN. *Quizas es nuestra carcelera.* [Perhaps she's our gaoler.]

DAME PHEMY. Are you hearing me? Queen Margaret hersel, asking for een o' you. Come on. Are you deef?

PETER *is watching her now. She turns to him.*

Christ save us, whit language dae black folk speak?

PETER. You're speaking to me in guid Scots, Dame Phemy, that's working fine.

DAME PHEMY. Well, *they* canny mak me oot! Look at them!

PETER. Would you like me to translate?

She wouldn't. She thinks she's got no alternative.

DAME PHEMY. Aye. On you go then.

She backs off, frustrated. PETER *comes closer to* ANNE *and* ELLEN. *He begins speaking in Spanish then it switches to English – but we should understand he's still talking Spanish.*

PETER. *Lo siento señoras. Es muy grosera.* Do you understand what she wants?

ANNE. No.

PETER. She's asking if you're royal attendants.

ELLEN (*indicating* ANNE). She…

ANNE *cuts her off.*

ANNE. Are we prisoners now?

PETER. No. You're welcome here. The King wants you to stay, here, as part of the royal household.

(*He points at* DAME PHEMY.) She wants a royal companion, to attend the Queen.

ANNE *hesitates then decides to risk it.*

ANNE. I'm the Lady Anne. I've attended the Princesses of Portugal and the infanta of Spain.

ELLEN. I'm her servant.

PETER. *Bueno. Momentito.*

He goes to DAME PHEMY.

That's the Lady Anne. She's been a royal attendant.

DAME PHEMY. Aye. She's the look.

A'right. I'll bring her to the Queen.

PETER. The lassie there is her servant.

DAME PHEMY. Oh there's nae room for servants. We're twae to a bed up there as it is. The Queen's ladies share the servants we have, there's nae room for mair.

PETER. I'll tell them.

DAME PHEMY. What we need is an annexe but they're a year behind on the building work as it is.

PETER *is already speaking again with* ANNE *and* ELLEN.

PETER. *Te convertiràs en compañera de la reina*. But there's no room for your servant. We'll have to find another place for her.

ANNE. We stay together.

ELLEN. This is the Lady Anne. The *Lady Anne*! She needs her *own* attendant, for her clothes, her water, her hair. She needs me.

PETER. There's servants in the Queen's rooms. She'll be cared for.

ANNE. I need the servant who knows me. She's my companion, always.

PETER *cuts over her.*

PETER. This is a good place for you, a high place, in the Queen's bedchamber. This morning you thought you might be killed. This afternoon you thought you were a prisoner. Now I'm telling you you can join the household of a queen.

We'll find your companion another place.

DAME PHEMY *is getting restless.*

DAME PHEMY. Can they nae mak you oot either? Come on, whit's keeping you, Peter Morian?

ANNE. How do I trust you?

PETER. It's a good question. Where were you before?

ANNE. In Bilbao.

PETER. Ah. I heard there was plague in Bilbao?

ELLEN. Yes. So we needed better luck.

DAME PHEMY. Hu*llo*?!

PETER. I came from Bilbao, to La Rochelle and nearly stopped in London. But something kept me moving north. I've found better luck here than any other city in Europe. I'm married here. I have great houses and farms. I sit by the King. If you can't trust me yet, you can trust *my* luck. Why shouldn't it be yours?

ANNE. Where are the Queen's rooms?

PETER. Why? You want to check out the view?

ANNE. Where are they?

PETER *points*. ANNE *looks, considering*. *She turns to* ELLEN.

You see?

ELLEN *nods*.

(*To* PETER.) Very well. Take me to the Queen.

ANNE *turns to* DAME PHEMY.

DAME PHEMY. Oh, she's coming, is she? Hurry up then, Her Majesty's been waiting this long while.

PETER. Another time you could speak to her in French. Since your Spanish isny up tae much.

PETER *is leading the* MUSICIAN *away.* DAME PHEMY *glowers after him.*

DAME PHEMY. Cheeky bastard.

She looks at ANNE.

C'est vrais? Vous parlez français? [Is that true? You speak French?]

ANNE (*disdain*). *Bien sûr.* [Of course.]

DAME PHEMY. Well, why did you no…?! Never mind. *Venez ici.* [Come here.]

(*As* ANNE *isn't moving.*) *Ici! Ici!* [Here! Here!]

DAME PHEMY *leads* ANNE *away.* ANNE *throws a look back at* ELLEN. ELLEN *waits.* DUNBAR *is still watching.*

DUNBAR. Well, whatever work they find for you dinnae try poetry. That's my advice.

ELLEN *obviously doesn't understand him. She tries to move away from him. She's looking round her, trying to work out where she is, but always looking back towards the Queen's rooms. He follows her, trying to get her attention back.*

You're a wonder. You're a window into a wide world. We're not fit to look at you and when we do we show ourselves up eh? But they'll still look. Oh God they'll look. The world's notice is something I canny catch and you canny avoid…

(*Thinks about that.*) Mebbe we should stick together, you and me.

I think we should.

And this is how we should start.

He gets in front of her, stopping her, he points to himself.

Dunbar, William Dunbar…

He points at her. She doesn't get it yet. He does it again. Slower, clearer.

Dunbar.

(*He points at her.*) You?

She gets it.

ELLEN. Ellen.

DUNBAR. Ellen.

She points at him.

ELLEN (*faltering on it a little*). William… Dunbar…

DUNBAR. That's right.

(*He points to himself again.*) Dunbar… Makar… Poet…

Chiel.

He points at her.

Quine.

ELLEN. Queen?

DUNBAR. No, quine. Bonny quine.

ELLEN *points between them.*

ELLEN. Makar. Chiel.

Quine.

Makar Dunbar.

Bonny quine Ellen.

DUNBAR. There you go.

There you are.

All the world is words.

Slowly he points at the bits of himself he names.

Een…

Neb…

Lugs and mou…

Oxter…

Wame…

Hurdies… taes.

She copies him, slightly more hesitant, repeating the words.

ELLEN. Een…

Neb…

Lugs and mou…

Oxter…

Wame…

Hurdies… taes.

DUNBAR. Wow.

You're a fast learner.

Alright.

Hullo…

Hullo, Ellen.

She gets it.

ELLEN. Hullo.

DUNBAR. Hullo, Ellen.

ELLEN. Hullo, William Dunbar… makar.

DUNBAR. Hullo. How you daein?

ELLEN. How you daein?

DUNBAR (*emphasising the crucial words*). I'm *daein fine*, Ellen. How are you?

ELLEN. Daein fine.

They laugh together in delight at the speed of their connection.

DAME PHEMY *is back.*

DAME PHEMY. So where am I supposed to put this one?

DUNBAR. Ask her.

PETER *is back on.*

DAME PHEMY (*to* PETER). She'll need to go in wi' the entertainers. We've nae need o' servants.

PETER (*to* ELLEN). *¿Puede cantar? Baile?* [Can you sing? Dance?]

ELLEN *is looking between them, confused.*

DAME PHEMY. I've pit twae o' the ither Moorish lassies in wi' the nursemaids, there's nae mair room there. Whit ither use is she?

ELLEN *suddenly turns on* DAME PHEMY, *making a point.*

ELLEN. Hullo. How you daein?

DAME PHEMY. Jesus Mary Mother of God!

This one can speak Scots!

DUNBAR. Aye.

ELLEN *points at herself, insisting on her identity.*

ELLEN. Ellen. Daein fine.

DAME PHEMY. Someone's makin a fool o' me.

(*To* DUNBAR *and* PETER.) Is it you?

DUNBAR. What can I tell you? She's a quick learner.

PETER *has realised this is* DUNBAR*'s doing.*

PETER. Mebbe she had a good teacher.

DUNBAR. Thank you, my lord. Thank you.

DAME PHEMY. Well, it doesny matter how quick she is. There's nae meat left in the household budget. She'll need to go intae entertainment.

PETER. I doubt she's trained as an entertainer.

(*Considering* ELLEN.) She's got something. She does, but I've no time…

DUNBAR. I've naething but time, my lord.

PETER (*considers a moment*). Alright, let's see what she can learn.

He gives DUNBAR *money.*

DUNBAR. *Thank* you, my lord! I won't let you down.

PETER *is leaving.*

PETER. She can stay in the musicians' apartments. Show her, Dunbar.

Make sure she has a place by the fire.

PETER *is leaving.*

DAME PHEMY. Oh, they're all getting a place by the fire! And a privy that doesny reek. Een o' the loons got a pearl the size o' a pigeon's egg, jist for standing aboot looking foreign. Nice work, eh?

She curtsies to ELLEN, *slightly sarcastic.*

Sorry, Lady Ellen. By your leave, Lady Ellen.

DAME PHEMY *is off.* DUNBAR *turns to* ELLEN.

DUNBAR. I'll show you where to gang…

She's not moving. She points up at the Queen's rooms.

Ah.

Window. The Queen's window.

ELLEN (*repeating the word*). Window.

ELLEN *waits, watching the window. He hesitates.*

DUNBAR. Well… your bed's through there when you're ready for it.

He gets her attention and mimes sleeping, indicating where to go. ELLEN *shows she understands.*

I'll… I'll see you the morra.

The morra.

ELLEN. The morra… William Dunbar.

ELLEN *goes back to watching the window as* DUNBAR *leaves.*

Queen's Rooms

JAMES *has come to* MARGARET *to spend the night. He's getting ready for bed.*

JAMES. Now… I know we haven't had the best day but… let's put that aside eh? It's important what we do here. It could be more than that, for both of us. Try and think of this…

(*He indicates the bed.*) This is where England and Scotland lie down together and hold each other…

'Stead of setting each other on fire and chopping each other's limbs off.

You and I save lives when we kiss.

We join together and that border of war dissolves as we do.

That's what I feel. That's what we show the world. And that's beautiful, Margaret.

You're beautiful. My bonny wee wife.

MARGARET. Why did you send the Lady Asquith away?

He doesn't want to deal with this but he knows he has to.

JAMES. Right… so.

I'll say what needs saying. You won't like it. I'm sorry for that.

MARGARET. Can you just answer the question?

JAMES. So you know I read your letters.

MARGARET *says nothing.*

Even the ones you… try to slip past me.

MARGARET. You've no right.

JAMES. You wrote to your brother. Prince Henry of England. You said I had no money.

MARGARET. I didn't.

JAMES. You said 'My lord the King may be poor in gold but he is a better fighter than any in Europe.'

MARGARET. That's a compliment. I was saying nice things about you.

JAMES. If I'm poor in gold, how could I pay an army? You said 'My lord the King is winning the war against the rebel Highlanders with his own sword.'

MARGARET. Well, you *are*. Aren't you? You told me you were…

JAMES. You're telling England half my kingdom lies undefended while I make war on the rest of it!

MARGARET. But you are winning the war against the rebel Highlanders, aren't you…?

JAMES (*cutting in again*). And you said I would always ally with France. Do you understand how *dangerous* that is to the balance of…

MARGARET (*cutting*). Where did I say that?!

JAMES. On page fucking two, where you said the only good thing about my dinners was the French wine! You're not stupid. You knew words like these could bring war.

MARGARET. Oh, don't be ridiculous.

JAMES. We need to look powerful and prosperous and strong enough to need no allies at all. Always, *always*! And *now* I've had to send the Lady Asquith back to England, for trying to smuggle your letter… Why are you writing secretly to your brother anyway?

MARGARET. If I write privately sometimes he writes back…

He's the only one who still sends me proper news from home.

JAMES. This is your home, Margaret.

She says nothing.

I'm sorry if you still don't feel that, but it is. I know we keep coming back to this but… If you just tried to learn to speak Scots…

MARGARET. Why? French and English are the proper royal languages.

JAMES. Not for *Scottish* royalty…

MARGARET (*cutting him off*). Well, I'm English royalty.

JAMES. So you are. Alright.

She says nothing, utterly miserable. JAMES *sighs. He kisses her.*

I'll come back another night.

MARGARET. I've been sick.

JAMES. You're ill?

MARGARET. No. I'm just…

My courses have stopped.

JAMES *takes that in. Then he is beyond delighted.*

JAMES. But this is the best news, the *best*… Why didn't you say?!

You've just made Scotland's future! Margaret, ask me for anything! Any favour. What do you want? A pony? Christ, I'll even send to fetch Lady Asquith back, ask for anything.

MARGARET. Truly?

JAMES. Anything.

MARGARET. I want you to stop going to Tain.

A horrible pause.

JAMES. Well, I have to…

Sweetheart, it's on the justice circuit. When I take the court round the country I have to go to…

MARGARET. Alright. Just don't visit your mistress, when you go to Tain.

JAMES. But…

Sweetheart, there's no another house big enough to shelter us all, have you *seen* the size of Tain? We canny bed the King's court doon in a byre.

MARGARET. You said I could have anything!

JAMES. But that's…

Margaret, Janet Kennedy is mother to my children…

MARGARET. And what am I?! What am I, now?!

JAMES. Don't…!

Trying to touch her, calm her.

MARGARET. Dear Christ, my rage is going to shake this baby out of me!

JAMES. Don't upset yourself. Sweetheart, you have to be careful.

At some point under this ANNE *comes into the room.* JAMES *does not see her.*

(*Checks himself.*) I'm sorry. It's hard, I know, but remember you're my *Queen*. You're the only queen I have.

MARGARET. You've no idea how to treat a queen. You never have had. The Lady Anne here knows me better than you.

JAMES *sees* ANNE. *He startles.*

JAMES. Jesus fuck!

MARGARET. We've only just met and already we understand each other.

Nous avons déjà des bonnes conversations, Anne, c'est vrais non? [We're already having great conversations, Anne, aren't we?]

ANNE. *Absolument raison.* [Of course.]

JAMES. Good for you.

Bien pour vous autres.

MARGARET. Go away, James.

JAMES. Well, let's see if the Lady Anne can make you happy.

But I don't suppose anyone could understand how to make you smile when this mood's on you.

MARGARET. I think Archibald Douglas could.

JAMES. What?

MARGARET. You heard me.

JAMES. You can't say that.

MARGARET. I can.

JAMES. Don't you even think of looking at Archibald Douglas.

MARGARET (*losing it*). If you can shove your annoyance up Janet Kennedy and any of the four hundred others that take your fancy then I can turn my head for Archibald Douglas!

JAMES. No if you want to keep it on your shoulders you canny!

ANNE *cuts over this. She's indicating* MARGARET*'s stomach.*

ANNE (*cutting him off*). *Ça suffit!* [That's enough!]

JAMES. Ah, God forgive me…

I'm sorry, Margaret.

Pause.

I'm sorry for all your unhappiness.

He leaves, fast, angry now. MARGARET *smiles at* ANNE.

MARGARET. *Personne à part nous*. [Nobody but us.]

ANNE. *Je suis heureuse*. [I'm happy.] I am so happy to be here with you, Your Majesty.

MARGARET. Oh thank God I have one person left who might understand me. Can you bear it here? It must seem so bleak after the palaces in Spain…

ANNE *is looking round critically but with some approval.*

ANNE. Yes, the towers are small, but they're in the French style, very fashionable.

She goes to the window, apparently admiring the view, but also signalling ELLEN *below.*

And you have this wild park beside the palace.

MARGARET (*uncertain*). The park of Holyrood, yes, but it…

ANNE (*cutting in, approving*). That's very much the fashion now. Do you keep it stocked with deer?

MARGARET. I think… I don't know. I hunt deer there sometimes, yes…

ANNE (*smiling*). But not for these next few months.

As MARGARET *looks blank.*

The baby!

MARGARET. Oh Mother of God…

She slumps in despair.

I won't be able to do anything! And he's just going to… gallop about. Shagging half the kingdom and sucking up their adoration like warm soup.

ANNE *considers her a moment.*

ANNE. How old are you, Your Majesty?

MARGARET. Seventeen.

How old are you?

ANNE. More than that.

My fate has whirled me round like… a stone tumbling off a mountain. I've lived inside an avalanche for days now.

But if God has a purpose for me then it must be here, now, with you.

I've been a teacher of royal children. I think I can teach you, Queen Margaret.

MARGARET. Teach me?

ANNE. I hope I can.

MARGARET. Teach me what?

ANNE. To get what you want.

MARGARET *thinks a moment.*

MARGARET. I don't know what I want.

ANNE. Then first I'll teach you that. What does Queen Margaret want?

MARGARET. I want him to put me first.

ANNE. He must. You're carrying his heir.

MARGARET. I want him to put me first because of *me*, not because of what's in my belly.

ANNE. Ah.

That's harder. But we can make that happen.

ELLEN *appears in the room. She's carrying one of* ANNE*'s bags.*

MARGARET. Who…?

ANNE *speaks quickly, dismissive.*

ANNE. My attendant.

MARGARET *accepts this.* ELLEN *is unpacking beautifying equipment, make-up, combs or similar.*

MARGARET. My attendants are all sneering Scottish slatterns, cousins to the King. I hate them all. I'll just stay in these rooms. They can't make me go out. There are some things, at least, they can't make me do.

ANNE. Oh but you should go out. A court needs to see its Queen.

She nods to ELLEN. *Quietly and smoothly* ELLEN *and* ANNE *move into grooming* MARGARET *under the rest of this…*

And we'll walk beside you. I have wonderful clothes, you'll see, we'll make a great display of it.

MARGARET. I'll get him to give me back the pearls, Janet custard-faced Kennedy's pearls. He thinks I don't know he took them but I know.

ANNE. Don't ask for jewels. Ask for land. An abbey. A hunting estate. Jewels can be stolen or lost. Land is power you can keep.

MARGARET *isn't really listening.*

MARGARET. You don't know what it's been like for me here…

He tricked me.

He lied to me.

When I travelled up to Scotland to be married he couldn't wait to meet me. He galloped down into Northumberland to greet me. When we reached Edinburgh he put me on his horse in front of him and we rode in like that, together. Everyone cheered. Everyone. That's what I thought he'd be like. That's what I thought being Queen would be like.

But it was just a show.

In just five years everything I thought I had has been taken from me.

ANNE. In just one week everything I thought I had was taken from me. We need to know how to make our own happiness.

ELLEN *joins in, smiling agreement at* ANNE.

ELLEN. Always. Wherever fate takes us.

MARGARET *suddenly exclaims,* ELLEN *has inadvertently tugged her hair or touched some sensitive bit.*

MARGARET. Ow! No. Stop crowding me!

ELLEN *freezes, looking to* ANNE.

I'm tired. I don't want this.

ANNE (*careful*). Forgive us, Your Majesty.

MARGARET. Oh God, my head's aching! Send your servant away.

ANNE (*quiet to* ELLEN). Do you have somewhere to go?

ELLEN. Yes but…

MARGARET. Oh my poor head!

ANNE *jerks her head urgently at* ELLEN. ELLEN *starts gathering up their equipment.*

ANNE. I know, Your Majesty. It seems as if this day began so long ago.

MARGARET *looks at her properly.*

MARGARET. Are you tired?

ANNE *slumps a little.*

ANNE. When the sun rose I was still on the ocean.

MARGARET *hears this.*

MARGARET. Oh, you're exhausted.

Oh, you poor thing. You poor darling thing. Come here.

She pulls ANNE *to her.*

There. There.

Oh, Christ save me, there's going to be a child. What'll I do?

ANNE. We'll help you.

MARGARET. Yes. Yes, we'll help each other, it's so good to have *someone*.

ANNE. I'll help you get everything you want. You'll see.

MARGARET. Just promise me you'll love me best of every creature that ever lived.

ANNE *laughs a little.*

ANNE. Oh just that?

MARGARET. I'm serious!

ANNE *is startled by* MARGARET*'s tone.*

Promise me you'll learn to do that. To love me above everything.

ANNE. Of course. You're my Queen now.

MARGARET. And you'll love no one, *no one*, better than me.

ANNE. No one.

ELLEN *is ready to leave. She and* ANNE *share another look, then she goes.*

MARGARET. Good. Let's sleep now. This day is done and dead and I despise it. But it brought me you. It brought me the dear Lady Anne who loves no one better than me.

ANNE. No one. I promise.

MARGARET *settles to sleep.*

ANNE *sits sleepless a moment, processing what she's landed into.*

ELLEN *is down below now. She sings quietly, looking up at the window. A Moorish ballad.*

ANNE *turns her head to listen. Then she turns away and settles to sleep beside* MARGARET.

Courtyard/Garden

Nine months pass. We see them pass as ELLEN *and* DUNBAR *rehearse a poem about the passage of time.*

DUNBAR.
Off Lenten in the first morning,
Early as the day up spring,
Thus sung one bird with voice up plain:
'All earthly joy returns in pain'

Under this we see a transformation. A year moves through and MARGARET*'s baby is born.*

Oh man, have mind that thou mun pass,
Remember that thou art but as
And sall in as revert agane:
All earthly joy returns in pain.

ELLEN *takes the pages from* DUNBAR. *She reads, hesitant at first but growing confident. At some point* PETER *is on, watching this 'rehearsal'.*

ELLEN.
Come never May… fresh green… young grass
But Januar comes all howling blast…
Was never…

She sticks on the word, DUNBAR *is prompting, urgent…*

DUNBAR. Drouth! Drouth!

ELLEN (*getting it*).
…drouth but aye comes rain:
All earthly joy returns in pain.

PETER (*to* ELLEN). Good! Good! Pitch it up. Louder. Straight back. Big voice.

ELLEN.
Her health returns aye in sickness,
And mirth turns aye tae heaviness,
In touns, in desert, forest, plain:
All earthly joy returns to pain.

Queen's Rooms

We hear a crying baby. MARGARET *is sick and weak.* ANNE *and* DAME PHEMY *are with her.*

The DAME *is talking quietly to* ANNE.

DAME PHEMY. *Voulez vous embrasser l'enfant aujourd'hui, ma dame?* [Will you hold the child today, my lady?] Just for a moment. It's been a couple of months and you've still not really…

MARGARET (*cutting her off*). I can still hear it! Tell them to take it further away. I can still hear it.

Is it dying?

Tell them to take it further away.

ANNE. Of course, Majesty.

She moves to do so.

DAME PHEMY. It might stop crying if you held it, Your Majesty.

MARGARET. No.

DAME PHEMY. Well… you do still need to get up, Queen Margaret, to greet the King's guest.

MARGARET. Everything still hurts.

DAME PHEMY. Oh I don't think so. You're all healed by this time, Your Majesty. Aren't you? And they're expecting you. Everyone's gathering to greet the King…

MARGARET. But he is back. Let him come up here and ask me to welcome *his guest*.

DAME PHEMY. Now… if I were you… I'd try and remember he's not long back from the war…

MARGARET. But he is back. Let him come up here and ask me to welcome the lords of Europe to *his* reception.

ANNE *cuts over this, taking control.*

ANNE. Are you cold, Your Majesty?

MARGARET. I'm always cold.

ANNE. It's warm outside. Warmer than in this cold stone room…

DAME PHEMY. I've put three braziers in here! I canny do more without the tapestries go up and roast her like a pigeon!

ANNE *shushes her, focusing on coaxing* MARGARET.

ANNE. I know, I know these have been terrible dark months. I thought they would kill us. The light shrank. The cold came. I looked out over the fields and the parks and I thought this was dark, dead land. All my joints went hard as the rocks in that dead earth…

But… look it's *growing again*. When the weak pale sun returned, this earth grew green. A miracle. Everything dead is coming back to life. Even the air is softer. We can move again. We can go out. I'll help you.

MARGARET (*cutting in*). I can't. Oh God, I'll never be whole again.

DAME PHEMY. You want to see the King? He'll be down there, any minute, looking for you.

MARGARET (*to* DAME PHEMY). You have a cross, horrible face and I don't want to look at it any more today!

A moment.

DAME PHEMY. Ken whit a skelp is, Majesty?

MARGARET. What?

DAME PHEMY. Micht cure whit ails ye.

DAME PHEMY *leaves.*

MARGARET (*to* ANNE). What was she saying?

ANNE *has no clue either.*

ANNE. Never mind her. But you do need to get ready. Your Majesty, please… Listen to me now. Listen to me!

You are the Queen of Scots! I'll find a moment, soon, a moment when everyone is watching you. You'll take your place beside him and I'll lay your baby, his heir, in your arms.

Then he'll see. Then the whole world will give you the status you deserve.

Trust me. Will you trust me?

MARGARET. Alright.

ANNE *starts to get* MARGARET *ready as we see –*

Courtyard/Garden

PETER *is talking quietly to* ELLEN. DUNBAR *hovers nearby.*

PETER. You've done this before. You've been performing poems for months now.

ELLEN. But this is for the King. And it's different, when they're all looking at me.

PETER. I've heard you. Dunbar's taught you well. You're ready.

DUNBAR. Of course she's ready.

PETER *takes* ELLEN *away or gets* DUNBAR *to back off.*

PETER. Listen… I know this has been hard. We've had our moments, eh? I know you'd rather have been with your lady in the Queen's household but you'll find a home with us in the end, you'll see.

ELLEN. I've learned the words.

DUNBAR. She has!

ELLEN. I like… the words but… maybe I just don't understand the point of this…

PETER. Of your performance? We're celebrating victory!

ELLEN (*cutting him off*). Of anything!

I just want to look about and see one thing that feels like mine…

PETER. Aye. Aye, I mind what that was like for me. The first months here, the sun was too pale, the air was too blue, the folk were noisy ghosts beyond understanding… but they have to be understood, how else can you eat and wash and find your way roond this dark place of cauld stanes?

ELLEN. Aye. Aye, that's what it's like.

PETER. But you *listened*, you grabbed for sense in their sounds like a hungry bairn trying tae catch icy fish with her hands… and look at you now. You mak me oot fine, eh?

ELLEN. Aye. I can.

DUNBAR. You know the words. Just say them like you say them to me.

PETER (*cutting him off*). I've got this, Dunbar. Give me a minute.

DUNBAR. Absolutely, excuse me, my lord.

PETER *ignores him again, talking only to* ELLEN.

PETER. You don't have to worry about the crowds today. They won't be there till the tournament, tomorrow. This is easy, a victory poem for the King and a few of his friends. A wee surprise to greet him. They'll love you. You'll see.

We were cold strangers you and me, but… slowly, slowly, a sleeping fish breathing in wee beasties, Scotland opened its mou and swallowed us up. And it's warm in here noo, eh? We're daein fine. You're daein *fine*.

ELLEN. Yes. Thank you.

DAME PHEMY *is on*.

PETER (*to* ELLEN). Look at you! Victory!

This is going to be good. *This* is going to delight the King.

PETER *starts getting* ELLEN *ready for what she has to do – pose, props, etc. – talking all the while*.

Right. He's close. He's on the Canongate, hear the horses? He'll come through. He'll introduce his guests. Greet the Queen…

(*To* DAME PHEMY.) Where's the Queen?

DAME PHEMY. Wha kens?

A moment.

PETER. Christ.

Right. It's fine, it's all fine. Just keep your eyes on me, I'll cue you to start the poem.

DUNBAR. Well, shall I tell her…?

PETER (*interrupts*). I'll tell her. Just stay out of the way, Dunbar.

ANNE *and* MARGARET *are on. Just making it in time.*

PETER. Over there please, Your Majesty. Just in time. He's coming.

MARGARET *goes to her place but* ANNE *checks in front of* ELLEN.

ANNE (*to* ELLEN). What are you doing? What have they made you do now?

PETER *is chivvying* ANNE *to her place.*

PETER. Over there! Over there! The King's coming! He's here!

JAMES *is on with* DONALD, DOUGLAS *and another of his entourage.*

Welcome hame, Your Majesty! Welcome hame!

JAMES. Thank you. Thank you, Peter. It's good to be hame. And I've brought a guest.

(*To* DONALD, *in Gaelic.*) *Thig a-steach, thig a-steach, tha e ceart gu leor…* [Come in, it's alright…]

(*To everyone.*) You all know who this is, Donald Dubh, heir to the Lordship of the Isles. Donald is our wee token of peace.

DONALD *is looking round, enjoying himself, confident.*

DONALD. *Chan eil mi cho beag sin, Seumas Stiùbhart.* [I'm not that small, James Stewart.]

JAMES. No, fair enough, no sae wee.

PETER. The whole nation thanks God for your victory.

The Lords of the Isles have lain down their weapons and now that Donald Macdonald is your hostage…

JAMES (*checks him*). Donald's my guest, Peter.

PETER. Of course, Majesty. Excuse me.

JAMES (*to* DONALD). *Seo far am bi an fleadh againn*. [This is where we'll have the feast.]

DONALD. *Ach nach bi sinn a' sabaid ri taobh a' chaisteil?* [But won't we be fighting beside the castle?]

DONALD *is looking round at the courtyard.*

JAMES. *Tha.*

You'll be fighting later. Tomorrow. At the tournament. It'll be great. I reckon you'll destroy all challengers.

Come into the hall now, come on, look here's my Queen to welcome you, let her serve you a drink.

PETER. But first a moment to welcome you home, Majesty. Victory herself will speak!

JAMES. Ah! Of course. Lovely. On you go then.

ELLEN *steps up, poses.*

ELLEN. See Victory!…
I am Victory… I greet my King with…
I am Victory!

She dries, watching ANNE *watching her. Holds the pose. Can't speak.*

JAMES. Is there more?

DUNBAR *tries to take it up.*

DUNBAR. See Victory! My doughty sword that…

PETER (*cuts him off*). We welcome Victory! And now the feast! Into the hall!

JAMES. Odd wee display there, Peter. Queen Margaret?

MARGARET *is smiling and talking to* DOUGLAS.

DONALD *is already walking to the hall*. PETER *stops him.*

PETER. The King goes first!

JAMES (*making a joke of it*). He still thinks he's King of the Isles.

(*To* DONALD.) Come on, Donald. We'll go in together.

(*Sees* MARGARET *and* DOUGLAS.) I'll escort my wife into the hall, thank you, Douglas.

JAMES *takes* MARGARET*'s arm and ushers* DONALD *off.*

ANNE *follows.* DAME PHEMY *last, throwing her jibe at* PETER.

DAME PHEMY. That went well, eh? Great entertainment, Peter.

ELLEN *has just stayed in the pose. Now she crumples.*

PETER (*to* DUNBAR). Rewrite the opening to the tournament fight. We won't be using her after all.

DUNBAR. Oh but…

PETER. Cut her out!

DUNBAR. But you canny jist…

I've been working on that for *months,* my lord. You canny have the whole thing new by *tomorrow*!?

PETER *isn't listening. He's already leaving,* DAME PHEMY *follows him, still amused.* DUNBAR *is momentarily beside himself.*

Oh Mother of God… the whole *thing*!

ELLEN. He just means my speeches.

DUNBAR. But that's… *all* of it!

God rot him! Peter the fucking Moor!

ELLEN (*chilled by* DUNBAR*'s tone*). He's tried to be kind to me.

DUNBAR. Oh you think? See what happens now, now you're nae use tae him. He'll kick me back on the street soon enough.

Do you know how long I waited at that gate there begging for an audience? All my skill, *all my skill*, all my great songs and poems and *still* I have to wheedle and caper and sweet talk just to give them the gift they dinnae even deserve, my words!

Oh God, I thought I'd found my way hame at last. This show… it brings me back beside the *King*! But now that bastard wants it new? For *tomorrow*?

ELLEN. Can you do it?

DUNBAR (*simple despair*). No.

No I canny.

Well. That's the end. The end of hope.

The end of Dunbar. Oh, sweet Mary, help me! What's my life to be now?

I should never have given up the chance of a Church job. Madness.

But I've too much imagination to be just a priest.

No priest can do what I do. They promise salvation, but I create understanding of sin. I've words for a'thing human, a mirror to our damaged souls. Priests promise eternal life, but *I* create it. When my words describe a mortal creature they will be seen, forever, as long as words are read. That's the power o' a poet.

I offer the gift o' posterity. Is that no worth a wage?

Songs? Songs are nothing, songs are easy. But you never see musicians begging at the gate eh? They don't even have to comb their hair. They can write seventeen lines that don't even make sense but if the rhyme's on the beat and they're wailing about love everyone will treat them as if they're touched with divine fire!

You think some waster strumming a guitar could stare into the abyss? You want social commentary, you want a view of eternity, you ask a fucking poet!

But they won't.

Will they?

ANNE *is on*. ELLEN *hesitates*.

ELLEN. I am sorry.

DUNBAR. Aye… aye… you said…

Well… there you go.

He starts to leave.

ELLEN. What are you going to do?

DUNBAR. Try and write it new.

ELLEN. But… you said it couldny be done?

DUNBAR. But I have to try. What else is there?

He's gone. ELLEN *turns to* ANNE. *She is relieved and happy to see her, expecting* ANNE*'s sympathy.*

ELLEN. *¡Todas están enojadas conmigo!* [Everyone is angry with me!]

ANNE. *Claro que si*. [Obviously.]

ANNE *has a jewelled cloak and some food.* ELLEN *is taking the food, picking at some of it, rejecting other bits as they talk.*

I can't stay long. Since the baby came she's worse. I can't anchor her to common sense. She's half mad every day of the week.

She gave me this. You can take it.

She drapes the cloak round ELLEN. ELLEN *is pleased.*

ELLEN. *Thank* you!

ANNE. Margaret doesn't always like too many people round her.

ELLEN. I know.

ANNE. I can see things aren't going well for you.

ELLEN. No…

ANNE (*cutting in*). But when she's in that mood she only wants me. Just me.

ELLEN. Alright.

Alright I understand.

I'll keep my distance again for a few days.

ANNE *says nothing.*

I understand. She still won't let you have an attendant in her rooms…

ANNE. She'll never allow that.

This is what I have to tell you. It's been months. I've tried everything. Everything I tried made it worse. She doesn't even want you walking beside us now.

ELLEN. But we make her look *good*, what does she think…?

(*Stops herself.*) Well. We've tried. We can't do more. It's time, isn't it?

ANNE. Time for what?

ELLEN. To start again. Remember when I was too scared to get on the boat at Bilbao? I'd no strength or hope left that day but you pulled me onto that ship. 'We *can* start again. We will!'

I'm stronger this time. There's no place for us here, not together, but, we still have our promise. 'As long as we have each other that's the only home we need.'

We'll find another place.

ANNE. I don't want to get back on a boat.

ELLEN. We don't have to. We could pay an English merchant. Someone will carry us south over the border.

ANNE. I don't want to go south. I've got a place here.

ELLEN. You just said. There's no place for me too. We have to leave.

ANNE. No.

ELLEN. What do you mean, 'no'?

ANNE (*bursts out with it*). *I've carried you half your life! Now will you get up and carry yourself?!*

ELLEN *can't speak from the shock of that.*

You can't ask…

It's hard here. Yes. But I found a place. You can't ask me to give that up. You should have tried harder.

Don't look at me like that. I'll still help you. But you have to try something else.

ELLEN. Like what?

ANNE. I can recommend you to one of the Queen's acquaintances.

ELLEN *doesn't get this at first. She doesn't react, trying to work it out.*

There are women, *wealthy* women in Aberdeen, Inverness, Dundee who would preen to have a lady like you walk beside them and raise them up.

And… well… you know, half the girls who were on the ship with us have accepted marriage.

ELLEN. What are you telling me?

ANNE. There's no way back, to where we were, but maybe you can still find a life here. I'll help you. A marriage to a man, with a little land, would give you safety. I think there may be some wealth in their strange, dark soil. I watch the crops and the cattle they carry up the Canongate. Poor stuff but their grain and greens keep well. A farmer with royal favour. You could do worse.

ELLEN *doesn't respond.*

I hear the Lady Gordon wants an attendant for herself and a wife for her bastard cousin. She'd have you in her household, he has land. Shall I speak to her?

ELLEN. 'As long as we have each other that's the only home we need.'

ANNE (*snaps again*). You're not a child, Ellen! Stop clinging to my skirts!

Look… we would still see each other… Lady Gordon comes to court.

ELLEN. I don't want that.

ANNE. Well you can't have what you want! And I can't get it for you! You have to make your own way, Ellen, it's time.

There are jewels on the cloak. You can…

That'll give you a start, whatever you decide.

ELLEN *can't answer.*

I have to go back to the Queen.

Let me know when you've decided what you want.

She kisses ELLEN. *She leaves.*

Then DAME PHEMY *is on, moving fast. She grabs at the cloak* ELLEN *holds and tries to pull it off her.*

DAME PHEMY. That's no yours!

This is the Queen's silk, no yours.

ELLEN. Give that back.

Gie me my claes!

DAME PHEMY. Your claes? *Your* claes? I'll say whit claes are yours, lassie. Peter Morian says you're tae find anither place, well you'll no be robbing the Queen's wardrobe on your way oot!

DAME PHEMY *has wrenched the cloak from her.*

ELLEN. Give it *back*!

DAME PHEMY *evades her and is gone.* ELLEN *stands isolated, full of her misery. The* MUSICIAN *is getting ready, tuning up, playing fragments of song.* ELLEN *moves closer to the music.*

ELLEN *starts singing along with the* MUSICIAN, *quiet at first, comforting herself.*

The royal party are coming on now, DONALD *first then* JAMES, DUNBAR, *then* MARGARET *and the rest. They stop, listening, as* ELLEN*'s song grows louder and more powerful. She hasn't seen this audience, she's singing only for herself, she's singing the song she shares with* ANNE.

She finishes. Applause. ELLEN *turns, startled to see them all.*

DONALD. *Bha sin brèagha. An cuala tu i? Àlainn.* [That was beautiful, did you hear her? Beautiful.]

JAMES. You're right, Donald. Beautiful.

He comes to ELLEN.

I haven't noticed you before.

DUNBAR *is in there.*

DUNBAR. The Lady Ellen will perform in the tournament with you tomorrow, Your Majesty. Peter will explain it. It's all prepared.

JAMES. Wonderful. We'll give them a good show, eh?

ELLEN *curtsies deeply.* JAMES *takes* MARGARET*'s arm and the royals move out.* DUNBAR *is triumphant.*

DONALD *comes to* ELLEN. *He bows before her.*

DONALD. *Nuair a bhios mi nam rìgh seinne tu dhomh a h-uile latha.* [When I am King you'll sing for me every day.]

DONALD *follows* JAMES *out.* PETER *is still considering* ELLEN *– he could be very angry.*

PETER. Fine.

On with the show.

BAM! Straight into –

The Arena

ELLEN *falls to the ground in the arena.*

ELLEN. No!… What are you…?! *No!*

But her attackers are already gone, somewhere in the dark a great door booms shut and locks.

ELLEN *picks herself up, shaken, terrified, and looks round the audience.*

We do not see any audience, no MARGARET *watching, none of the royal court. We are with* ELLEN *in the arena and we are the only audience at this point.*

No. This is *no right*! I'm no supposed to be here.

There's been a mistake.

PETER *enters, taking up a commanding position.*

PETER. Edinburgh! Are you ready?! Are you ready for a real show?!

DUNBAR *is on, taking up his position.*

ELLEN. What is this? What's happening?

DUNBAR. You're the star of the tournament, Lady Ellen, just as I promised.

ELLEN. But… *No!* This is the arena! This is where they fight!

From his position PETER *is addressing the crowd.*

PETER. Prepare to see a fight to the *death*!

DUNBAR. Do you understand your duties?

ELLEN. No! What…?

DUNBAR. Every tournament has the brawest lady as its judge.
Your face brought you here, all that beauty has its price.
Now you have to determine the worth of a man.

ELLEN. You bastard, you *bastard*! You lied to me!

PETER. My lords, ladies, *mesdames et messieurs*! I give you… the man with no name!

*'*JIM*' is thrown into the arena. This is* JAMES*, but disguised so as to be unrecognisable. He looks frail and weak. He gets up, seeming to try and orientate himself, frightened.*

ELLEN. No! He can't fight! He's just a poor wild creature, from the forest! This isny right!

PETER. Can this wee creature win the greatest prize?

ELLEN. What's the prize?

DUNBAR. You are. You're the greatest prize.

ELLEN. No. No, I canny do this.

PETER. The Queen of the Fight will decide the champion!

DUNBAR *indicates* JIM.

DUNBAR. This wee article is a just common wild little Scotsman.

(*To* JIM.) What are you fighting for, wee man?

JIM. My bairn… I've a newborn bairn in the forest… he needs…

DUNBAR (*cuts him off*). There you go! Motivation! Will it save him?

Is one wee Scottish scrapper fit to take on the most dangerous men in Europe?

PETER. Queen of the Fight! Call your warriors!

ELLEN. *No!*

JIM. Just dae it.

A brief hesitation, then ELLEN *goes for it, seeming upset, but trying to play the game.*

ELLEN. Let the games begin!

DUNBAR. Nice. Clichéd but classic.

PETER. *Mesdames et messieurs!* My lords and ladies, I give you –

The seven-times winner, in this very arena! A trail of bodies follows him across Europe! Danish Dan!

DANISH DAN *enters and parades his splendour.*

DANISH DAN. *Jeg en er mester!!* [I am the champion!!]

DANISH DAN *sees* JIM, *he laughs.*

They want me to fight *that*?!

PETER. Fight! Fight! Fight!

PETER *encourages applause.* DUNBAR *steps back, pulling* ELLEN *out of the way.* DANISH DAN *is squaring up to* JIM. *He swipes at him.* JIM *just manages to dodge, swipes back.* ELLEN *gets between them.*

ELLEN. Stop! That's it!

(*Pointing at* JIM.) He won!

DUNBAR. What?

ELLEN. You said I declare the winner. I declare the wild man.

DUNBAR. Drama and comedy, ladies and gentlemen, drama and comedy! Very good!

(*To* ELLEN.) But it's a fight to the *death*, Your Majesty!

ELLEN *is advancing on* DANISH DAN, *keeping eye contact with him.*

ELLEN. Dan? Is it Dan?

DANISH DAN *is distracted. She's close, touching him.*

DANISH DAN. *Ja… hvad er det?* [Yes… what is it?]

ELLEN. Why are you doing this, Dan?

Then, quick as she can, she shouts to JIM, *who is behind* DANISH DAN.

Stab him now!

JIM *runs from behind to stab* DANISH DAN *in the neck.*

He falls, choking. JIM *is nearly crying.*

JIM. I'm sorry, I'm sorry, I'm sorry…

The death looks realistic but there is a notable absence of blood.

ELLEN. You had to. He'd have killed you.

DUNBAR. But *he'd* have made a better show of it.

DUNBAR *is examining the body with distaste.*

Aye, he's deid.

PETER. The wild man has won!

ELLEN. He's won! He's won!

ELLEN *and* JIM *are awash with relief, smiling at each other.*

PETER. But that was a *coward's* trick!

He encourages boos.

We need a champion! Not a coward! Bring on the next fighter!

ELLEN. *What?!*

JIM. Oh, for fuck's sake!

MAURICE THE MUTILATOR *enters and parades for the crowd.*

PETER. From Paris to Padua, he's run them through and made fricassee of their livers…

From the fighting fields of Flanders, I give you –

Maurice the Mutilator!

MAURICE. *Ik zal hem vermoorden! Ik zal ze allemaal vermoorden!* [I will kill them! I will kill them all!]

PETER. Fight! Fight! Fight!

JIM *lunges at* MAURICE, *their weapons lock together.* JIM *is yelling in fear. They both end up on the ground. They roll and then* JIM *is struggling free in flailing panic and* MAURICE *is lying still.* JIM *is hyperventilating.*

MAURICE *doesn't move. He's fallen on his own weapon.*

Again the movement is very real but there's no blood.

DUNBAR *edges over. He calls up to* PETER.

DUNBAR. Well, he's deid but he fell on his own sword, he basically killed himsel, eh?

ELLEN. It's a win.

PETER. *Was* that a win, ladies and gentlemen?

ELLEN. Yes! Yes it was! The wild man has won! He's beaten all the other fighters in the arena!

DUNBAR. Mebbe… but we've still no had anything I'd call entertainment.

ELLEN *just stares at him.*

JIM. Aw, you're fucking kidding me. You're *fucking* kidding me.

PETER. We've still not found a true *champion*! Let's see if this wee skelf can stand up to a *real* wild man. Can he face the untamed beast that is a wild Gael?! A deadly Highlander! No prison can hold him!

DUNBAR. And here's a few lines to tell you what I know of the man…

JIM (*cutting him off)*. Aw Christ, just get it over with!

For the first time ELLEN*'s reaction is slightly off.*

ELLEN. No… he… the makar has…

JIM (*cutting her off)*. Yes! Do it!

PETER. Bring on the next fighter!

BOOM! A great door somewhere in the darkness bangs open. DONALD *stalks in, looking like a ferocious killer.*

He roars a challenge in Gaelic, deafening.

JIM. How about I just kill mysel?

ELLEN. You can do this.

JIM. No I fucking can't! Look at him!

ELLEN. You can beat him. *You have to!* Kill him! Kill him! Go on!

DONALD *runs at* JIM *and the fight begins.*

JIM *starts off clumsy and frantic. He escapes death with flukes and apparently lucky dodges.*

You're a wild man!

And JIM *is looking like a better and better fighter all the time. Fighting back properly now, holding his own.*

You're an army all on your own!

And JIM *is fighting like a champion, like a hero, he drives* DONALD *back and back…*

You've a bairn and you'll hae a hundred mair. As strong as you! Every one! Kill him!

JIM *surges forward.*

DONALD *falls.*

JIM *kills him.*

A silence. He looks at ELLEN.

You won. You won. You won!

I declare the wild man the winner! I declare the wild man has won!

PETER. The wild man has won! We have a champion! We have a *true* champion!

JIM *seems close to tears. He drops his weapon.*

Then the music starts, a surging, exciting beat of rising triumph, as ELLEN *walks to* JIM. *The music stops as she reaches him…*

PETER *is kneeling now.*

Wild man. You are a worthy winner. Tell us your name.

In a dramatic gesture, JIM *pulls off his mask and reveals himself as* JAMES.

JAMES. I am James Stewart! King of Scots! And my sword alone can hold this land against any attack!

The music surges. ELLEN *crowns* JAMES. *Then* JAMES *puts robes on* ELLEN, *dressing her as a radiant queen.*

A display. ELLEN *is the centre of it and* ELLEN *looks* amazing*!*

They all pose…

Then there's a lighting change, the fourth wall is restored, suddenly they're all a group of performers backstage, applauding each other. The FIGHTERS *in particular have markedly different personas.*

Well done, everyone! Well done! I think they liked it!

FIGHTER. Sounded like they did.

JAMES. Course they did! Well done, Donald.

In reply, DONALD *swings a weapon at* JAMES. *It connects.*

There's no edge on that, Donald, you canny kill me.

DONALD (*furious*). *Blaigeard! Leag thu sìos mi*! [You bastard! You knocked me on my arse!]

JAMES. I warned you! I said I might knock you down if you wereny quick!

DONALD. You promised I'd die on my feet. Like a warrior…

JAMES. Christ, look at him, he does still want to kill me. Come here, Macdonald. I love you. Well done.

JAMES *forces* DONALD *to hug.* DONALD *suffers this but is not appeased.*

(*To* DUNBAR.) They liked it, didn't they? Do you think they liked it?

DUNBAR. Why are you asking me?

JAMES. What's up with you?

DUNBAR. Everyone came off the lines.

PETER *snorts.*

JAMES. Did we? No really, I just improvised a bit, didn't I?

DUNBAR (*to* PETER). I was waiting. I was *waiting* for the fucking cue and you just…

PETER (*cutting him off*). There were too many words, Dunbar.

JAMES. We didn't miss much though, did we?

DUNBAR. Oh you know, just one wee poem might have been good eh?

JAMES (*realising*). Jesus, we cut over the poem!

(*To* ELLEN.) Why didn't you stop me?

ELLEN (*thrown*). I…

JAMES. We cut over the poem!

DUNBAR. It's fine, it's fine just…

JAMES (*cutting him off*). Do you know though, we kind of had to, because the pace is really really roaring up at that point, I mean the third fight's coming. I think it's a good cut. Another time I think we need less at the front, a simpler set-up, straight to the fight…

PETER. Aye.

DUNBAR (*cutting in*). Oh aye, aye, because that's the show we want to put on for the world eh? Blood, mayhem and a thousand Scots cheering it on. That's a national character we can all be proud of, eh? Let's get batshit drunk and nut each other into oblivion. The French ambassador canny get enough of that eh? God forbid we should dilute that caricature with a wee bit of *poetry*.

JAMES. Any fool can write poems. I wrote poems.

DUNBAR. You wrote poems?

JAMES. Not any more.

DUNBAR. Were they any good?

JAMES. No.

DUNBAR. So any fool can't write poems, eh?

JAMES. Are you calling me a fool?

A beat.

DUNBAR. No, Your Majesty, I'm sorry I…

JAMES *turns from him*.

JAMES (*to* PETER). The wild man, though, that is…

We *have* to do that again! I felt…

PETER. Aye, that worked.

ELLEN. The poem could go later mebbe.

DUNBAR. Ellen, stop it, just don't…

JAMES. Yes, later. After the show?

PETER. That makes sense. Save it for the smaller audience, at the feast. I don't think we need you in the show itself, Dunbar.

ELLEN. Oh but…

PETER. It was great wee story. Canny take that from you…

ELLEN. The audience *loved* it!

PETER. The front of the arena loved it.

But they couldny even hear you past the middle rows.

DUNBAR. Middle rows are where the money sits!

PETER. Enough, Dunbar!

JAMES. I'll hear your poem later, how's that?

DUNBAR *can't speak. He just bows. The crowd is still roaring.*

Listen to them! We have to go out again.

PETER *is rallying the performers.*

PETER. Back out there! In character, everyone, in character! Maurice! Channel that inner mutilator!

PETER *and* FIGHTERS *are off as* ELLEN *goes to* DUNBAR. JAMES *is waiting for her, impatient.*

ELLEN. You were good… really… it…

DUNBAR *stops her.*

DUNBAR. *Don't!* Just… don't. It's fine. It's all fine.

JAMES *interrupts, grabbing* ELLEN.

JAMES. Come on! Queen of the Fight! You're with me!

ELLEN. What…?

JAMES. Come on! You're the *prize*!

Scene instantly transforms back to –

Arena

JAMES *takes the adulation of the crowd.* ELLEN *is beside him.*

ANNE *is on, she's carrying the baby.* MARGARET *is close behind her.*

ANNE *urges* MARGARET *forward.* ANNE *is holding the baby, ready to give it to* MARGARET. ANNE *tries to pitch above the noise, to* JAMES.

ANNE. Your Majesty! Your Queen is here, your heir the Prince…

PETER *cuts over her.*

PETER. Your winner, James Stewart King of Scots!

JAMES *has barely noticed* ANNE *or* MARGARET *as the crowd cheer again. He's loving it, soaking it up.*

JAMES. Did I win?!

The audience roars back.

Did you see me win?

Another roar.

Should I claim my prize?!

The biggest roar of all. JAMES *pulls* ELLEN *forward and raises her arm.*

The Queen of the Fight, ladies and gentlemen!

He kisses ELLEN *then he pulls her off. A few bawdy shouts follow him.* ANNE *steps forward and tries to give* MARGARET *the baby.*

MARGARET *pushes her away.*

PETER. My lords and ladies, wine and food are available for all, I'm sure His Majesty will return to us in due course but until then… God save the King!

We just see MARGARET, *shocked and humiliated, and* ANNE, *trying to soothe the baby, as the lights fade on the arena.*

The baby starts to cry.

Blackout.

ACT TWO

James's Rooms

ELLEN *stands near the door, a little wary.*

JAMES. It's just show. All of this is just for show. I don't expect you to…

You can go. Of course you can go. But I'd like you to stay.

She hesitates.

Stay for one drink?

She steps further into the room.

Good! Come away and sit doon then.

She hesitates then does so.

ELLEN. Is this what the world is like for you, everyone cheering? Everyone full of gladness jist tae see you wave?

JAMES *laughs.*

JAMES. I suppose. Aye.

ELLEN. I thought I hated their eyes on me but… when they look at me like *that*…

JAMES. Like you're a miracle? Well why wouldn't they? That's what I see.

She's looking sceptical.

You dinny understand that, dae you? But to me… you come from a legend, you come from places I can only imagine…

The King canny leave the kingdom.

I'm building ships. The ocean is the future. But they won't let me sail in them.

ELLEN. Surely you can dae what you want.

JAMES. You'd think. Royalty's not a' that Queen Ellen. Sorry. When I think of all you might have seen…

Have you been tae Venice?

ELLEN. Of course.

JAMES. Why of course?

ELLEN. I attend…

(*Small hesitation.*) I attended the Lady Anne. All European nobility find their way tae Venice sooner or later.

JAMES. Oh rub it in, why don't you. Where else have you been?

ELLEN. What dae you want, the story o' my life?

JAMES. Aye. That'll do.

ELLEN. My hale life?

JAMES. Just gie me the geographical highlights.

ELLEN *starts to make a game of this, performing it.*

ELLEN. I was born in Granada cam swift tae Seville. Stamping my wee legs and yelling for meat.

I ate too much of a'thing, my faither sent me tae service, cauld een on me, shouts at me, tears flawin oot o' me, I'm slipping in sorrow on sleek marble flaers…

Fountains and frescoes and dancing white mares.

Then I cam tae my lady, my best freend, my sister, Lady Anne's pu'd me wi' her tae Lisbon tae France…

Dusty roads, cyprus trees, sweet smelling leaves…

We drink fire wine in Venice. We gang whooping through Florence. We burp royal bairns and we grind royal spice…

Cinnamon, cardamom, nutmeg and mace…

We're the fiercest the brightest, we dazzle three kingdoms. Then Lady Anne fancies marriage, so that's what we dae.

She finds us a braw laird, wi' braw men aboot him, we're merriet together on the very same day.

Candles and feasting and birling and song.

Side by side merried ladies, oor new life began…

…But then death creept oer the country and gobbled oor luck.

Oor braw hoose is empty. Sorrow breaks in and robs us, we're lost and we're widowed and oor new wealth's taein awa…

We watch the grey ocean, the Lady Anne wants tae cross it, I'm nae caring, nae thinking, I walk on the boat…

JAMES. And then…?

ELLEN. And then here cams pirates! Fierce Scottish pirates! And there's screaming and slashing and we're all like tae dee!

And so we did.

We were all kilt deid and born new in Edinburgh toon.

JAMES. You've had some adventures.

ELLEN. I have.

JAMES. A hale life.

ELLEN. And now this is my different life.

JAMES. How're you finding it?

ELLEN. Better… today.

JAMES. Aye. You've fair found your voice, eh?

ELLEN. This is how the Queen o' the Fight aye talks, didn't you know?

JAMES. Peter told me you were no performer. Look at you.

ELLEN. I'm no.

I didny want to be… at first…

JAMES. How aboot now?

ELLEN. Perhaps I can dae it, a little.

JAMES. Perhaps you can dae it? You should see yoursel.

ELLEN. The show was the maist… the *best* thing!

JAMES. That story we told…

ELLEN. It was real!

JAMES. You felt that?

ELLEN. Aye! You were that poor wild loon and oh God I needed you to win…

JAMES. I was out of myself…

ELLEN. Aye.

JAMES. You were a queen.

ELLEN. Was I?

JAMES. Didn't you feel it?

ELLEN. Aye.

JAMES. But this can't end well. He's just a wild creature from the forest and she's a queen.

ELLEN. She's no, nae really.

JAMES. Queen of the Fight.

ELLEN. They saved each other.

JAMES. You think they can go on saving each other?

ELLEN. For a little while.

JAMES. Maybe they can.

They touch each other and then ELLEN *feels the chain he wears and pulls away.*

ELLEN. It's true!

They told me about this! I thought it was a story! It's true!

He doesn't answer.

Show me!

Slowly he takes off his shirt and reveals the chain wrapped round his body.

She touches it.

She examines where it's marked his skin.

Why do you wear a thing like that?

JAMES. To feel it.

To remember.

I killed my faither.

ELLEN. I know. Everyone knows. I don't know how. It was in battle?

JAMES. Aye.

ELLEN. Was it terrible, to cut him down?

JAMES. I imagine it. I wasny there.

ELLEN. If you wereny there how did you kill him?

JAMES. I led the army.

ELLEN. But… I heard you were a boy?

JAMES. Fourteen.

ELLEN. And they let you lead the army?

JAMES. No but, they fought in my name so…

ELLEN. Did you ask them to?

JAMES. I didny stop them.

ELLEN. Could you have stopped them?

As he doesn't answer.

I should go.

JAMES. Aye.

Why should you go?

ELLEN. The Queen.

JAMES. But you're the Queen.

(*As she doesn't respond.*) Aye. Aye. The Queen.

I've sent my bairns away, out of Edinburgh. They want me to call them bastards but I won't dae it. My Alexander will be Archbishop of St Andrews and my wee Meg will have her ain court around her, as long as I hae breath.

ELLEN. How old is Alexander?

JAMES. Fourteen. *He'll* see the world. That I can mak happen.

Queen Margaret came here a bonny child and she never grew up. She doesny seem tae want tae grow a woman's wisdom. She's a bairn yet.

So what does that mak me? A man that put a baby into a child. Hell isnae deep enough.

The wild man is free of a' that. He jist has the green forest and the fight.

ELLEN. I don't think you wear that chain because you killed your faither.

JAMES. The wild man doesny wear a chain at a'.

ELLEN *touches the chain again.*

ELLEN. Does he know why the King has this about him?

JAMES. The King broke a promise to his mother.

The King doesny confess his sins any more. He just adds weight on the chain and learns to carry it.

ELLEN. Well we all carry weight like that…

(*She's taking some of her clothes off.*) But look. There's no way to tell.

(*Pointing.*) Here's where my mither gripped my hand when she left the world… nae mark…

Here's the place that brak first when my faither pushed me awa tae find anither hame… nae mark…

And here's where I held my ain heart in my ribs to stop it bursting oot when my Lady Anne walked awa frae me to follow the Queen o' Scots…

We're all marked.

Only a new bairn has nae scars.

He sees marks on her though. Touches them.

JAMES (*realising*). Oh, you had a child.

You've lost your bairn too.

ELLEN. I telt you. Sorrow broke in oor braw hoose. The Lady Anne's man was taken, then mine… and then death cam back again for my bairn. She had a moth's life. Soft and quick. The scars she left are deepest but even they're nae on my skin.

I remember.

Why do you need a chain? Don't you remember your own life?

JAMES. I'm sorry.

ELLEN. What are you sorry for?

I've a new life now. Stop being sorry. Tell me a story instead.

JAMES. The Queen of the Fight and wild Jim can't live till morning.

ELLEN. No.

They live in so much danger.

This is their last night…

He moves closer to her, looking for permission. He kisses her.

Courtyard/Garden

The next morning. It's the aftermath of a wild night of drinking. Litter of food and drink, people collapsed on the ground. DUNBAR *is slumped beside a bottle.* DAME PHEMY *comes on, she stares round the mess.*

DAME PHEMY. Ah God…

Someone else can deal wi' all this. No. Find yoursel another place Phemy, you're done here.

ANNE *is on.* DAME PHEMY *sees her.*

What do you want? You gonny pick up a broom?

(*As* ANNE *says nothing.*) No. Nae mair am I.

DAME PHEMY *exits.* ANNE *goes to* DUNBAR *and shakes him awake. She points to where* JAMES *and* ELLEN *exited.*

ANNE. Is she still with the King?

DUNBAR. Didny see her come back.

ANNE. Then it's done.

DUNBAR. Aye. The whole world saw.

ELLEN *comes on. She's startled and a little embarrassed to find* ANNE *there.*

ELLEN. What are you daein here?

ANNE. Are you alright?

ELLEN. Of course! Why wouldn't I be alright?

ANNE. I thought…

She can't say what she thought.

ELLEN. The King is kind.

DUNBAR. Is he? Oh is he though?

ANNE *cuts in.*

ANNE. What did he give you?

ELLEN. What?

ANNE. This will be a short season. You need to get a good crop. Jewels to last a lifetime. Or land, get him to give you land.

ELLEN. I'm not a *beggar*.

ANNE. You need to take what you can, as soon as you can.

We hear MARGARET *shouting, or see her above.*

MARGARET. I can't! I can't!

ELLEN. I think your Queen's looking for you, Lady Anne. Should you no be about your work?

ANNE *leaves.*

DUNBAR. Did he show you the famous chain? That never fails him, that'll get you any lassie, he's wearing his pain ootside his skin and you get tae stroke it.

I need to tell you…

I've been thinking, all night… See what I'm trying to say… Once the King's done wi' you *no one* else will have you.

(*Hastily.*) I mean they will! After they saw you in the show yesterday… Christ if you wereny under the King's protection half the world would be trying to have you already, but no one is going to offer marriage, I mean you'll likely be rich enough, aye, the King's generous but… do you *want* that? A rich hoor till you're too shrivelled up tae be any kind of hoor?

So I was thinking… We get along well enough, eh? I mak you laugh. We want the same things… alright maybe I do fancy the idea of sharing your gold but we can mak so much more of it before you're done. You could still own half of that. No other man'd gie you that. And if there were bairns… well I'm no saying I'm expecting that but, I'd acknowledge them, you know? They'd be my ain, well hopefully they would be my ain but… och I'm getting ahead o'mysel.

She says nothing.

Look… I know it's not what you maybe wanted most but I'm just saying think about it.

A wee back-up plan.

What do you say?

She's just staring at him.

What's that look? I canny read you. What do you think?

He moves towards her.

ELLEN. *Don't.*

DUNBAR. What?

ELLEN. We've still a performance to get through. Until then I don't want to talk to you.

She's leaving.

DUNBAR. What the fuck…?

That is a good offer, a *kind* offer, from a man that *cares* about you. You dinny need to be looking at me like that! There's nae need for…

Aye, fuck off then! Hell mend you!

Queen's Rooms

MARGARET *is cradling the baby. She turns as* ANNE *comes in, she's in a terrible state.*

MARGARET. Where were you?!

ANNE. I… you were sleeping… you never wake so early I…

MARGARET *holds out the baby to her.*

MARGARET. I can't. I just can't. They've left me with him. How could they just…

ANNE *sees the baby is really ill.*

ANNE. Oh! Oh he's so ill…

MARGARET. They said I had to hold him. She said I had to sit here, alone, and hold him. Because he came from my body.

Because only my touch can keep him in the world now. But why should I hold him if he wants to go to heaven?

ANNE. When did he get so ill?

MARGARET. *When you were away!*

ANNE. I'm sorry. I…

MARGARET. If I hand him to you, will he die?

ANNE. I don't know.

MARGARET. Because I don't want to hold him.

Take him.

ANNE (*hesitates*). But…

MARGARET. *Take him!*

ANNE *takes the baby.*

Is he dead?

ANNE *can't speak.*

Is he? Is he dead?

ANNE *holds the baby a moment.*

ANNE. I think he's dead.

MARGARET. Are you sure?

It's over then. It's over. Oh, Anne, it's been a terrible night. They woke me in the dark and you were gone…

ANNE. I'm so sorry.

MARGARET. I just wanted it to end. He kept breathing and breathing, little pants and gasps like a dog, on and on. I thought it'll stop soon. It has to stop soon. But it didn't.

ANNE. I'm sorry.

MARGARET. That's a terrible thing to think. I'm a monster. Does it sound like I wished him dead?

ANNE. No.

MARGARET. I didn't want him to die.

ANNE. He's in heaven. A pure child. He's flown straight to heaven.

MARGARET. I'd rather he'd stayed alive. I really would.

ANNE. Of course. But he's with God.

MARGARET. Did he…?

Did he die when I let him go or was he dead already?

Did we kill him?

ANNE. I don't know.

MARGARET. You shouldn't have taken him from me.

ANNE. But…

MARGARET. Why did you take him from me?! I told you what she said!

He died when you touched him. Didn't he?

ANNE. He…

I don't know.

He was very sick.

MARGARET. But he was still alive. Oh, what have we done? What did you make me do?

ANNE. Queen Margaret… there was nothing you could do…

MARGARET. Yes there was, they told me what to do. If you'd been here you'd've heard them. If you'd listened to what they said you'd never have let me do that! Why weren't you here?!

DAME PHEMY *is on. A* PRIEST *hesitates behind her.* DAME PHEMY *takes in the scene.*

DAME PHEMY. Aw no, aw, say we're no too late, is he deid? Is the wee soul away?

MARGARET *is now ramping up her genuine distress.*

MARGARET. She took him. She took him. I couldn't hold him.

DAME PHEMY. Oh, oh darling, oh wee pet, it's alright now. It's alright. Come here to me.

DAME PHEMY *gathers* MARGARET *up*. MARGARET *breaks down in her arms*.

MARGARET. I never wanted him to die.

DAME PHEMY. Oh no, sweetheart, no. Course you didny. Who's saying such badness?

ANNE *is just standing, holding the dead baby.*

MARGARET. She took him.

DAME PHEMY (*to* ANNE). Put the wee Prince doon now.

ANNE. I didn't…

DAME PHEMY. Put the bairn doon! Now!

ANNE *puts the baby down. The* PRIEST *goes to him*.

ANNE. We should lay him out, somewhere else, the Queen is too upset to…

DAME PHEMY (*cutting her off*). I'll see to the Queen.

MARGARET (*to* DAME PHEMY). Make her go away!

ANNE. Alright.

I'll leave you now, Your Majesty. I'll come back to you with water and fresh clothes…

MARGARET. No. *No!* You can't touch me. You can't *touch* me! You've death in your fingers.

And you scold me.

And everything you tell me to do has come to *dust*.

And you *left* me!

And I don't like your face!

ANNE. Margaret…

MARGARET (*shouting her down*). I don't like your face! I don't like your face! I don't like your face!

DAME PHEMY. Well, that's you telt, eh?

(*She advances on* ANNE.) We'll need to find you another place. Eh, lassie? Come away now.

She moves ANNE *away from* MARGARET.

ANNE. The Queen will need…

DAME PHEMY (*cuts her off*). You don't think I can give the Queen what she needs? No. You've never thought much of me at all, have you? I saw the look you gave me, the day you arrived, priced every stitch on my back.

Well, I'll tell you, my lady muck, I know more about this town and this court and what Queen Margaret needs than you'll ever discover.

So *back off* and find yourself another place to sit today.

ANNE *leaves.*

DAME PHEMY *is helping the* PRIEST *lay out the baby.*

In another space, DUNBAR *and* ELLEN *are performing his poem.*

DUNBAR.
Into the dark and drublie days,
When sable all the heaven arrays,
With misty vapours, clouds, and skies,
Nature all courage me denys,
Of songs ballads, and of plays.

ELLEN.
When that the nicht does lengthen hours,
With wind, with hail, and heavy showers
My dull spirit will crack for sure,
My heart for langour does forloir,
For lack of summer with his flowers.

DUNBAR.
I walk, I turn, sleep may I nocht,
I vexit am with heavy thocht,
This world all oer I cast aboot,
And ay the mair I am in dout,
The mair that I a cure have socht.

The scene transforms to a funeral. JAMES *and* MARGARET *kneel at the altar and then watch as the tiny coffin is carried away.*

JAMES *speaks quietly to* MARGARET.

JAMES. If God's willing to bless us we'll make another child.

MARGARET. I don't want to.

JAMES. I know. But that's our job.

Then it's another day and the funeral party is reforming as guests at a rehearsal dinner.

Great Hall

DUNBAR.

And then says Age, My friend, come near,
And be not strange I thee require,
Cum, brother, by the hand me tak,
Remember you have count to mak,
Of all the time you're spending here.

ELLEN.

Syne Death casts up his yettis wide,
Says 'Past this entry you'll abide,
Albeit that you were ne'er sae stout,
Under this lintel shall you lowt,
There is nane ither way beside.'

MARGARET *is leaving the funeral with* DAME PHEMY. ANNE *stands lost and uncertain a moment, then she leaves in another direction. All others are now in the rehearsal.*

DUNBAR.

For fear of this all day I drowp,
No gold in kist nor wine in cup,
No lady's beauty nor lovers bliss,
Can spare me frae the thocht o'this,
How glad that ever I dyne or sup,

ELLEN.

Yet when the nicht is growing short,
It does my spirit sum part comfort,
Of thocht oppressed with icy showers,
Cum, lusty Summer with your flowers,
That I may live in some disport.

JAMES. That's beautiful.

Murmurs of agreement.

PETER. It's no very cheery though, is it?

DUNBAR. I was *asked* tae reflect on grief and loss, I was *commissioned* to commemorate sorrow and…

JAMES (*not hearing this, to* ELLEN). What are your thoughts?

What does the Queen of the Fight think?

ELLEN. About the poem?

JAMES. Aye.

ELLEN. I think it's beautiful.

DUNBAR. Thank you.

ELLEN. But… I'm no sure if it's right. For this show. Now.

PETER. *Thank* you!

ELLEN. You said…

(*Hesitates, to* JAMES.) Is it alright to repeat what you said?

JAMES *smiles at her.*

JAMES. Sweetheart, of course. You'll say it better than me.

ELLEN. The whole of Christendom is watching Scotland, again. We had a hope, a bairn that could have ruled two kingdoms. That bairn is deid.

The nobles of Europe and the ambassador of England have come to see if Scotland's hope is deid too. They've come to see if we still stand strong.

We can't show them oor grief.

We can't show any doubt.

JAMES. That's it.

PETER. *Aye!* That's it. No poetry, not at this feast.

JAMES. Aye, that's best. Thank you, makar. Let's get on with the rehearsal. Donald, you're up…

DONALD *doesn't move.*

MARGARET *and* DAME PHEMY *come on. Again* ANNE *trails some distance behind.*

Margaret! Fantastic, just in time. You look gorgeous by the way.

He kisses her hand.

(*Showing her her mark.*) So you'll be coming to here… and Donald will be just here.

(*Looks round for* DONALD.) Donald, what are you doing? Get over here.

Slowly, reluctantly, DONALD *takes his place.*

(*To* PETER.) Is this the right place? Do we need to leave space for the disappearance?

PETER. No, no, we're saving the disappearance for after the tournament.

JAMES *and* ELLEN *go with* PETER *as he shows them where the trick will happen.* DUNBAR *is glaring after* ELLEN.

DAME PHEMY. What's that face aboot, makar?

DUNBAR. Nothing.

DAME PHEMY *sees where he's looking.*

DAME PHEMY. Oh aye. I ken whit it's aboot…

PETER (*explaining*). So explosion, Lady Ellen *vanishes*… then she reappears there…

(*Points.*) …crowned as the Queen…

MARGARET *too is glaring at* ELLEN.

MARGARET (*cutting in*). That's *after* the tournament. Why is she here now?

JAMES. She's *attending* you, sweetheart, we've been over this.

DAME PHEMY. I can attend the Queen.

PETER. Nae offence, Dame, but naebody wants to see you modelling a basket of summer flowers.

DAME PHEMY. Oh is that right?

JAMES (*to* DONALD). Let's walk through what we need to do here.

DAME PHEMY (*to* PETER). They'd rather see you cutting a caper roond the hall, would they?

JAMES. Everything here is for show. That's what I wanted to say to you, this isny real, it's just ceremony, it's a…

(*Searches for an explanation.*)… *'S e direach sgeulachd a tha seo, chan eil e fìor.* [This is just a story, it's not real.]

Everyone understands it's no real but they'll get what I'm saying.

DONALD. You're saying you're strong enough to beat any one of them because a man like me is your prisoner. You're saying you defeated my uncles, you broke their ships, you brought down their towers, you took their lands and told the world my title did not even have meaning any more. There are no Lords in the Isles. My father was the last. You're King of all of Scotland now. And as I am a royal man, like you, a man of honour, like you, I admit that. I'll show that truth.

JAMES. Lovely.

DONALD. But you cannot say, you can never say that I will not be Lord of the Isles again.

JAMES. Wouldny dream of it.

(*To the others.*) So Donald kneels here… Donald?

DONALD. Aye?

JAMES. This is when you kneel down. You spread your arms like this and stretch your neck for my sword.

DONALD. Aye.

JAMES. So…?

Do you want to do that?

DONALD *hesitates, then he does it.*

Alright…

(*To* MARGARET.) My sword's at his neck, I'm really going to heft it up, you know? I'll make it look real. So the quicker you can get in through that door there…

MARGARET. It'll depend what I'm wearing.

JAMES. Could you maybe… wear something shorter? Easy to run in?

MARGARET. I'll be wearing something *new*.

JAMES. Good. Well. Something to think about when they're sewing up the hem.

So you rush in, fast as you can get here because I'm *really* takin his heid aff if you dinnae. And you say –

'King James, I beg you. You're a great king, strength alone can offer real mercy. Spare this man, King James, for your Queen's sake.'

Got that?

MARGARET. King James, I beg you. You're a great king, strength alone can offer real mercy. Spare this man, King James, for your Queen's sake.

JAMES. Fantastic! And I say –

'I'll spare him then. Only for the Queen's sake.' I'll walk over and raise you up…

The Queen of the Fight strews our path with flowers…

ELLEN *takes the flowers and throws them down as* JAMES *walks over and raises* MARGARET.

And then we're done!

You can get up then, Donald.

DONALD (*getting up*). Why is it a show?

Carson a tha sinn ag innse sgeulachd? [Why are we telling a story?]

JAMES. Because I don't actually *want* to kill you, you arse!

DOUGLAS *has come to take* MARGARET*'s arm –* JAMES *sees.*

Douglas, what are you doing?

MARGARET. He's *attending* me, dearest. We've been over this.

DONALD. You wouldny kill me. If we had a real fight, with real blades, I think I'd kill you, *Seumas Stiùbhart.*

JAMES (*distracted*). I don't think we…

DOUGLAS (*cutting in*). Will *we* have a fight?

DOUGLAS *is acting up for* MARGARET*, flirting with her by goading* JAMES.

JAMES (*irritated now*). *What?!*

DOUGLAS. We could do that, you and me. It'd be a better show?

JAMES. We're *demonstrating* the unity of Scotland. How does me fighting you…?

MARGARET (*cutting in*). Oh but I'd like to see that!

(*To* DOUGLAS.) Would he beat you? He'd probably beat you.

She starts repositioning the rehearsal.

(*To* JAMES.) And then he'd be down like this… and I'd throw myself over him, to beg your mercy…

She's draping herself over DOUGLAS*, who is loving it.*

JAMES. Margaret, get up…

MARGARET. But it would be a much better…

JAMES. *Queen Margaret, get up!*

A nasty pause.

You know what you're doing, Donald?

DONALD. Aye.

JAMES. Then we're done here.

(To himself.) Christ.

PETER. Then the feast is brought in. Then it's the dance.

MARGARET. Well, can we have dancing now?

JAMES *(still angry)*. The Queen wants dancing. Give the Queen what she wants.

PETER *(shouting off)*. Music!

Music.

MARGARET *starts dancing with* DOUGLAS. JAMES *watches for a moment, fuming.*

Suddenly DUNBAR*'s running into the middle of the dancing.*

He starts dancing and performing his poem.

DUNBAR.
My lairds and gallants tried tae dance,
They skipped a new yin oot o' France.
And though they craved the ladies' praise
The ane foot gaed ay onyways
And tae the tother would nocht agree.
Shout out, 'Tak up these staggering knights!'

He's imitating the others dancing throughout, getting laughs.

A merrier dance micht nae man see.

Then he starts to caper wildly.

Then cam in Dunbar the makar:
On all the floor there was nane frackar,
And there he danced with capers quick,
Tripping like a sow that's sick
To charm the ladies, they tell me.
He hoppit like a waggling prick,
A merrier dance micht nae man see.

Then he's on DOUGLAS*, imitating and widely exaggerating* DOUGLAS*'s dancing style.*

Than cam in the Douglas maister
Ane hommilty yommeltye stumbling dancer.
Like a stirk staggering in the rye,
His arse gave mony a hideous cry.

He's indicating that DOUGLAS *is farting.*

Dunbar the fool said, 'Waes me,
He's shat himsel! Oh fye, Oh flee!'
A merrier dance micht nae man see.

DUNBAR *is pantomiming horror at the idea* DOUGLAS *has shat himself. Everyone is laughing except* MARGARET.

DOUGLAS *storms off.*

JAMES. Oh Archie… Archie, man, you're no *leaving* us are you?

He's handing money to DUNBAR.

MARGARET *stands, abandoned.*

DUNBAR. I can bring doon ony chiel on earth!

JAMES (*to* PETER). That was good entertainment. What would you call that?

PETER. A good flyting.

JAMES. Archibald Douglas has been flyted! What do you say, Queen Margaret?

MARGARET *won't answer him. She leaves,* DAME PHEMY *following.*

I think that was great entertainment.

PETER. That's the rehearsal over, ladies and gentlemen. Two days to the tournament, stay sharp everyone, stay sharp.

PETER *is moving the other performers off.* JAMES *is moving off,* ELLEN *following –* ANNE *intercepts her.*

ANNE. Ellen. I want to speak to you.

ELLEN (*surprised*). What about?

ANNE. Not here…

ELLEN. It'll need to wait. I'm with the King.

ANNE. But…

ELLEN. You'll need to wait, Lady Anne.

ELLEN *follows* JAMES.

DUNBAR *is moving off, counting the money* JAMES *gave him.* DAME PHEMY *steps in his path.*

DAME PHEMY. The Queen wants a word wi' you, Dunbar.

She pulls him off.

ANNE *waits.*

After a moment DONALD *comes to sit near her, drinking. He offers her drink but she refuses. They wait. A long cold wait.*

Over this we see –

Queen's Rooms

MARGARET *and* DAME PHEMY *are on* DUNBAR. *He is uncomfortable and very nervous.*

DUNBAR. Queen Margaret… Your Highness… I never meant…

DAME PHEMY. You never meant *whit*?

DUNBAR. I would never have done that, if I'd any idea, I'd nae idea to upset you or…

MARGARET. How am I upset?

DUNBAR. By that… cheeky… poem. I…

DAME PHEMY. Which poem?

DUNBAR. At the dance I…

MARGARET. Oh was that about *me*?

DUNBAR. No, no, of course it wasnae…

MARGARET. I thought that was about bad dancers and Archibald Douglas.

DUNBAR. Aye! So…

MARGARET. Why should I care what you write about Archibald Douglas?

DAME PHEMY. Are you saying the Queen cares for Archibald Douglas?

MARGARET. Are you accusing me of adultery?

DAME PHEMY. Is that no treason?

MARGARET. It is.

DAME PHEMY. Whit's the penalty for treason?

MARGARET. He'll be burnt alive.

DUNBAR. What the… actual… *whit*?!

Your Highness! Your merciful Highness! I've done nothing but praise you! Ever! Ever!

MARGARET. He wrote praise poems for my marriage.

DAME PHEMY. I heard them. They were shite.

MARGARET. No. No, that's harsh.

They were… derivative.

DAME PHEMY. That's the word.

DUNBAR. The praise was sincere! My… worship… is true!

DAME PHEMY. Worship?

MARGARET. Worship.

DAME PHEMY. Oooh that's a big word.

DUNBAR. It's… it's true. I worship you, beautiful Highness.

MARGARET (*to* DAME PHEMY). He's sticky. Slimy.

DAME PHEMY. Sleekit. But he can deliver a good flyting.

MARGARET. Oh yes, *those* poems have always been good.

DUNBAR. You… you want a poem from me?

DAME PHEMY. Mebbe.

MARGARET. If you do what we ask you'll be well rewarded.

DUNBAR. And if I dinnae I'll be burnt alive?

DAME PHEMY *and* MARGARET *speak almost at the same time.*

DAME PHEMY. Yes.

MARGARET. No, just…

DAME PHEMY *checks her. They glare at each other.* DUNBAR *starts to smell the truth.*

DUNBAR. Hud on! Hud on a wee minute! You want to commission me? You want me tae gie you a piece of my work? And you're *paying* me?

MARGARET. If it pleases us.

DUNBAR. For fuck's sake! For fuck's *sake*!

DAME PHEMY. You're talking with your Queen!

DUNBAR. How could you no jist ask nice? Eh? What's all this… 'burnt alive for treason' carry-on?! There was no fucking *need*…

MARGARET. You'll be well paid.

DAME PHEMY. But we'll give you the words.

A beat.

DUNBAR. No.

No I'll no dae it. Use your words? I wouldnae stoop.
I wouldnae fucking *stoop*!

A letter, aye, a legal petition, sure, but a *poem*. My words are *mine*! If I start doon that road I am *deid*. I am nothing! When I start trying to please and appease, my voice is just whining in the reeds. *I* am a good gale off the sea, a east coast wet shout that scorns flattery, you canny tame a wind like that, you canny just snap your fingers…

DAME PHEMY *takes out money and shows it to him. It stops him. He hesitates, terribly torn.*

No. No, I'd rather sit begging at the gate all my days. The whole pile of you have bounced me aroond like a game of ball and never known my worth. Nae mair! You canny buy what isnae in my soul.

MARGARET. But we'll…

DAME PHEMY *checks* MARGARET, *fixed on* DUNBAR.

DAME PHEMY. No. I doot not but that's true. We'll settle for that, Dunbar, all that's in your soul and nae mair. Not a word you canny speak with your whole heart. That's a promise.

Is that a promise, Queen Margaret?

MARGARET. Of course.

DUNBAR. Alright then.

He snatches up the money.

Courtyard/Garden

ANNE *and* DONALD *are still waiting.* ANNE *looks at* DONALD *a moment, studying him.*

ANNE. *Culpo al mar…* [I blame the sea…]

I blame the sea, I do. I had taken ships before but this was… Just… the water… no sight of rock or tree or sand or roofs. Water all round us, it heaved and rolled and roared with spray.

And we jumped and tossed for day and days, like corn tossed in a cloth to lose its skin. I lost everything.

I lost the memory of life before.

I lost the hope that we would ever arrive anywhere…

That's what the sea does.

It's the salt I think.

Salt dries everything up.

(*Looking at* DONALD.) What's your reason?

DONALD. *Chan eil cuimhne agam ciamar a bhios-mi, mi fhìn. Chan eil fhios agam cò mi…* [I can't remember how to be myself. I don't know who I am…]

ANNE. You're too young to be so lost. I'm too young to be so lost… I have to begin again. We have to begin again. But it's exhausting, giving birth to yourself, over and over… I want to stop…

DONALD *starts speaking under* ANNE, *echoing her words in Gaelic, speaking at the same time but at his own pace.*

I could swallow a hawk, a hare, a hunting dog. They'd never find my soul. They'll run in my empty insides forever, howling…

DONALD (*same time*). *B 'urrainn dhomh seabhag a' shlugadh, no geàrr, no cù seilge. Cha lorg iad m 'anam gu bràth. Ruithidh iad nam corp falamh gu bràth, a' caoineadh…*

ANNE. I'm a cat without a hearth, I slink from shadow to shadow, shivering, looking for a place to rest, a slice of sun that no one will kick me from, where I can close my eyes and just be sleep…

DONALD (*same time*). *'S e cat a th 'annam gun teallach, bidh mi a' sleamhnachadh bho sgàil gu sgàil, a' gairisinn, a' lorg àite airson fois, sliseag grèine nach toir duine breab dhomh, far an urrainn dhomh mo shùilean a dhùnadh agus dìreach a bhith nam chadal…*

ANNE. And in that helpless thoughtless warm moment I will turn my head to any hand that strokes me, I am so cold, and so tired…

DONALD (*same time*). *Agus anns a 'mhòmaid sin, bhlàth, gun smaoin, gun chòmhnadh, tionndaidhidh mi mo cheann gu làmh sam bith a tha còir dhomh, tha mi cho fuar, 's cho sgìth…*

ANNE. If I could walk hame I would dae it. But I don't know where hame is… now.

DONALD. A green hill.

They're looking up towards Arthur's Seat, the hill in the park next to Holyrood Palace.

ANNE. I see one.

DONALD. Aye.

ANNE. Mebbe you should go.

DONALD. Aye.

DONALD *gets up and leaves.* ELLEN *is on.*

ELLEN. Alright. What do you want to say to me?

ANNE. I want to get married.

ELLEN *takes that in.*

The King will give you any favour now. Ask him this favour for me.

ELLEN. What about the Lady Gordon's bastard cousin?

ANNE *doesn't respond.*

Oh is he taken? Are you too late?

ANNE. Find me a man with land.

ELLEN. A wee laird?

ANNE. But I want a choice. I want to choose my own wee laird.

ELLEN. Course you do.

I don't know, Lady Anne, I'd need to warn your suitors that you're awfy picky. I'd need to tell them you don't like your friends to walk too close and you've no love of public entertainment.

ANNE. You could tell them I've got good common sense between my ears and not a pudding made of dreams.

ELLEN. I could tell them you snore on winter nights like a little piglet gargling in beer.

ANNE. You could tell them at least I keep my feet sweet and I'll never shove my dirty toes up their nose and wake them with the reek.

ELLEN (*complete change of tone*). Don't do this.

I could ask the King to let you join me, as my attendant…

ANNE. No!

I need another beginning. I've only one more left in me.

I want to marry.

ELLEN *feels that. A moment while she covers her reaction.*

Can you arrange this? Soon?

ELLEN. Oh it's the work of a day, Lady Anne.

ANNE. Good.

Well, you know where I'll be.

ANNE *leaves.* ELLEN *watches her go.*

Courtyard/Garden

Two days later. JAMES *brings two* FARMERS *on.* ELLEN *follows with* ANNE.

JAMES (*indicating* FARMERS). Lady Anne, these men are high in my favour.

ANNE. I'm glad to hear it.

JAMES. They have land and they'll have more soon, or one of them will, the one you choose. A wedding gift from the Crown.

(*To the* FARMERS.) Off you go then. Woo her.

FARMER. Aye but there's a dowry too, eh?

JAMES. What?

FARMER. You said it's no just land, you're throwing some cash in with the deal too eh?

ANNE. Not him.

FARMER. Whit?!

JAMES. Next suitor.

TURNBULL *fumbles a bag open, showing* ANNE.

TURNBULL. Right so… you might want to know about the earth so I've brought this here. It's, eh, it's good dark earth.

ANNE. What does it grow?

TURNBULL. It grows a wheen o' oats. It's no too claggy see, if you squeeze it, it'll still break to crumb but it'll hold a spring shower and it'll no crack in a frost.

ANNE *is touching the earth, smelling it.*

ANNE. Oats? What else?

TURNBULL. We get a great crop of onions, kale, but mostly it has the sweetest grass, we've got the fattest yows and a muckle herd of black kiy we took frae…

(*Checks himself.*) We, eh… found them, down in Northumberland.

The grass we feed them is fu' o' clover.

ANNE *turns to* JAMES.

ANNE. Him.

The other FARMER *starts to protest.*

FARMER. But I've no even…

ANNE *cuts him off.*

ANNE. Did you bring earth?

FARMER. No but…

ANNE *touches* TURNBULL.

ANNE. Him.

When can we get married?

JAMES. Congratulations, Turnbull!

The other FARMER *is leaving.*

FARMER. I came all the way frae Hawick for that? That wasny fair at all.

JAMES. The priest's waiting for you by the chapel, Turnbull. But tak a moment.

He steers TURNBULL *closer to* ANNE.

ANNE (*confirming his name*). Turnbull.

TURNBULL. Turnbull of Teviot Haugh. Pleased to meet you. The place is no that big, the hoose I mean. It's a bit poky. I was thinking of building it new. Seeing as you're used tae better.

ANNE. Good.

TURNBULL (*can't believe his luck*). Christ, look at you!

(*To* JAMES.) King James, I'd follow you doon a wet hill and through the back door of hell!

JAMES. Glad to hear it.

TURNBULL (*to* ANNE). I'll mak the hoose bonny for you. I promise.

ANNE. Good.

TURNBULL. Aw this is the *best* day. 'Mon then, you heard the King, the priest's waiting.

JAMES. I'll tak you through. Your bride will follow.

ANNE. I'll be there directly.

TURNBULL *goes to kiss* ANNE, *hesitates about how to do it, gives her a smacking kiss on the cheek and hurries off after* JAMES.

ELLEN *and* ANNE *are left.*

I can't stay here, with you.

ELLEN. Why not?

ANNE. I can't fall again. I can't fall further.

And I still think you might fall.

ELLEN. You want me to fall.

ANNE *is suddenly warm, urgent.*

ANNE. No. Oh no. Be a queen forever. Be *Queen* forever. Look at you. *Look at you!* Show them, Ellen. Show them who you are.

But I'm tired.

ELLEN. Fine. Leave me then.

ANNE. If you ever need a place…

ELLEN. Why would I need to come find you in a muddy field?

I won't be at the wedding. We're getting ready for the tournament.

I've given you wedding gifts.

ANNE. Thank you.

ELLEN. Goodbye, Lady Anne.

A moment between them.

ANNE *leaves as* JAMES *is on.*

JAMES. Never seen a man so happy.

ELLEN. It's all gone then.

JAMES. What's gone?

ELLEN. Everything of my life before. I've lost it or given it all away. There's only my life with you left.

JAMES. Well is that no enough?

She doesn't answer straight away.

I need you. The job of King is too great for one man to carry without love.

ELLEN. I know.

JAMES. Then know your worth.

He kisses her.

PETER *is on, supporting* DONALD. DONALD *is a bit drunk but mainly exhausted and dishevelled. He hasn't slept for days.*

Christ, look at the state of him. Is he going to be ready for the show?

DONALD. James Stewart, you call me a traitor. Over, and over and *over* again. Traitor. Traitor. Traitor.

So *why don't you kill me*?

PETER. We need to get some food in him.

DONALD. *Mura h-urrainn dhomh sabaid leig dhomh bàsachadh.* [If I can't fight you I'll die like this.]

ELLEN. Do you think he really wants to die?

JAMES. Aye. I think he really wants to die.

PETER. So let him die fighting.

JAMES. What?

PETER. The show. Let him fight you with a real sword. Use real blades.

JAMES. I'd kill him.

PETER. That's what he wants!

JAMES. No, I mean I'd kill him really quick. He's no bad but he couldny scratch me.

PETER. So let him bring a couple of friends.

JAMES. That would be fucking dangerous though.

PETER. Fucking dangerous is what we're after! King James, no king, no king in all of Europe would fight three men with real blades. Imagine when word of that got out.

And everyone in Europe is coming to this show.

JAMES. They'll see what I dare do to defend Scotland!

Bidh mi a 'sabaid ribh… Are you hearing me?… *Bidh mi a 'sabaid ribh.*

In the arena. With real swords. Real blades, Donald…

ELLEN. How will the crowd know the blades are real?

Someone needs to bleed.

Someone needs to be cut.

JAMES. Well, I'll no put them down without they bleed.

ELLEN. Before that, so the crowd know to be afraid.

I should get…

JAMES *cuts her off.*

JAMES. No!

ELLEN. I could be careful, I could judge it so I wasny hurt too bad.

JAMES. I said no!

They'll know enough when they see me at my work. They'll see the truth then.

Donald, I promise you. *Tha mi a' gealltainn dhuit.* I *promise.*

DONALD. I'll fight you?

JAMES. Yes. Yes.

DONALD *struggles up.*

DONALD. Alright then.

JAMES. Christ, he's freezing.

ELLEN. Here, I'll get him into the kitchen, I'll feed him by the fire. Come on, Donald.

ELLEN *helps* DONALD *off.*

PETER *is looking at* JAMES.

JAMES. If it's real… then this is between me and God. If I win, if the wild man can win, I can win any fight. That's what I'll know. That's what they'll all see.

God will help me win any fight.

PETER. Aye but…

DAME PHEMY *is on. He stops as he sees her.*

JAMES. Yes?

DAME PHEMY. A word. Frae the Queen.

JAMES. Aye. On you go.

DAME PHEMY. Alane.

JAMES. What's it about?

DAME PHEMY. About your wee show.

JAMES. If it's aboot the show then Peter stays.

DAME PHEMY. He can listen. But he's no telling you what's tae happen, no this time.

PETER (*laughs*). Well, if I could dae that…

JAMES. If the Queen wants tae talk to me, she can…

DAME PHEMY. She sent me. We thought I'd say it better. Clearer.

JAMES. I'm all ears.

DAME PHEMY. She'll no be coming.

JAMES. What?

DAME PHEMY. Tae your fight, tae your feast, she'll be in her rooms. She's no coming oot.

JAMES. She has to come oot. Half of Europe's here! What does she think it'll look like if she…

DAME PHEMY. She thinks it'll look like she doesny care to be with you. And what chance of an heir then? What chance of a new babe that could sit on the thrones of Scotland and England?

JAMES. You tell her…

(*Getting himself under control.*) You tell her there'll be six of my best men kicking in the door of her rooms and carrying her out if she doesnae…

DAME PHEMY. Oh you'll nae dae that. That's nae your style at a'.

JAMES. *Try me!*

DAME PHEMY (*continuing, unperturbed*). Just as you'll nae kick doon her door any night soon and throw her on the groond and roar your husband's rights in her royal face. You wouldny dae that.

JAMES. Of course I wouldny…

DAME PHEMY (*cutting in*). Which is the only way you're getting an heir. As things stand.

A moment.

PETER. What does she want?

DAME PHEMY. It's no jist her. It's what half the world wants. You're a good king, the best we've known. You've gied us peace but now you need tae gie us…

PETER. What?

DAME PHEMY (*still just to* JAMES). Reasons tae still love Your Majesty!

Look what you're *daein*. Just what your father did.

A good king should hae nae favourites. A good king wouldny shame his royal wife so!

Jist try and look as if you keep God's law. That's all we're asking for.

PETER. Who's 'we'?

DAME PHEMY. There's folk that love you that feel themsels forgotten, Majesty, that's the truth! Will you no even listen to me any mair?

JAMES. Of course I'll listen.

DAME PHEMY. *You know me*. I was born to three cauld rooms and fields of weed and stane. But I fought that fate. I caught mysel a canny laird. I pushed him up every ladder and intae every royal hall. I put him beside you and I've kept him there. I ken every coin you spend, I balance every book and I clear every clogged drain and I fix every fractured achette. I have no place to sit but never mind, I canny stop tae sit. I've climbed up frae dirt and noo I cling.

And nae higher will I climb. Holding on taks all that's in me.

I accept that.

As God has gifted me let me no ask for mair.

But…

There's those that have climbed oer me, kicking me in the mou as they used me for a ladder…

Jist as others have climbed to sit where your own wife should be.

PETER. The King honours Queen Margaret in every…

DAME PHEMY (*to* JAMES, *blocking* PETER). I am nae talking tae yon!

JAMES. Tell me what the Queen wants.

DAME PHEMY. Tak your eyes off that *woman*. You dinny even need tae send her awa. Jist… lower her… bring her doon.

JAMES. Bring who…

DAME PHEMY. Oh you know fine well who I'm talking about, Jamie!

Your Majesty.

Sorry.

You can have your fight, the great show, that… 'entertainer' can dae whatever you want in that. The Queen will watch and smile like it's nae bother tae her.

But after that, *after that*, that… *woman* will not sit at your table. The Queen will sit one side of you and my lord and I the other, as it's aye been, as it's *aye* been, Your Majesty.

And then we'll hae a… a praise poem… to the Queen.

PETER. Who's daein that?

DAME PHEMY. Makar Dunbar will dae that, Your Majesty.

PETER. We'll want sight of that.

DAME PHEMY *ignores him.* JAMES *holds out his hand.* DAME PHEMY *hesitates, then hands over the poem.* JAMES *scans it.*

DAME PHEMY. He's a trick of catching the mood I think, Majesty. It'll dae the job it needs tae.

After this we want Makar Dunbar brought into the royal household. He should have a place beside you, always. The Queen might like tae hear his words from time to time.

JAMES. And if I dae a' this, the Queen will… forgive me?

DAME PHEMY. She'll smile her love like summer sunlight for a' the world tae see.

JAMES. Alright.

DAME PHEMY. Aw, bless you, King James, *bless* you.

I'm so glad. I'm *so* glad.

I'll go to tell the Queen. Wait till you see how we've dressed Her Majesty, you'll need to hide your een, the splendour o' her will blind us all.

Thank you.

DAME PHEMY *is hurrying off.*

PETER (*the poem*). What does it say?

JAMES. I'm going to let him say it. She's right. This will work for Margaret.

PETER. But what does it say?

JAMES. We need an heir, Peter. Scotland needs a living heir.

PETER *just waits for a look at the poem.* JAMES *hands it over.*

It's another piece of the show! That's all. I want no argument from you! The makar will speak in the hall to please the Queen and that's an end to it!

JAMES *leaves.*

PETER *stands, reading the poem, processing all he's feeling.*

The Arena

ELLEN *walks out into the arena.*

A HUGE roar goes up. 'Queen of the Fight, Queen of Scots!' They're chanting it.

ELLEN *stands, proud and regal, receiving the adulation.*

This time we see JAMES *guiding* MARGARET *to her place in the audience, watching.*

JAMES *goes to* ELLEN.

He starts to take off all his royal regalia. The crowd is going nuts as ELLEN *helps him remove his royal robes. Underneath he's dressed as the wild man.*

ELLEN, *in full regal splendour, faces him.*

ELLEN. James Stewart, King of Scots, are you ready?

JAMES. Aye.

ELLEN. Where are my warriors?

DONALD *enters the arena, swinging his sword.* JAMES *and* DONALD *take up fighting positions.*

Only one will live. Show me my champion!

Music begins. JAMES *and* DONALD *start to fight.*

Just at the beginning it looks choreographed, on the beat of the music, but DONALD *breaks this first, slashing at* JAMES *in earnest.*

Then everything is chaotic and ugly, a real fight.

ELLEN *is moving round the fight, watchful, looking for her chance.*

The men push across her path.

JAMES (*to* ELLEN). The fuck you doing? Get out of my way!

ELLEN *has hold of a weapon. She raises it, showing the crowd.*

ELLEN. The blades are real.

She cuts herself, showing them.

The blades are real! Scotland, look what your King risks in your name!

The crowd goes nuts.

DONALD *roars a rallying call.*

DONALD. *A-nis! Thig a m'ionnsaidh!* [Now! To me!]

Two more men burst into the arena.

JAMES (*to* ELLEN). Get out of the way!

ELLEN *is jostled and goes down.* JAMES *is fighting all three men. He takes one down.*

The crowd is going mad.

JAMES *has one man down now he takes out another.* DONALD *is coming for him.*

It looks as if JAMES *is going down but he springs up, sending* DONALD *sprawling.*

DONALD*'s on the ground.*

JAMES *holds his sword to his neck.*

Do you want to live? Do you?

DONALD. I can't. I can't live with your sword at my neck.

Cur crìoch orm ma-thà, a bhlaigeard! [Put an end to me then, bastard!]

JAMES. No. Find your own death. I'm done with you.

There's a chain or rope on the ground (or wherever it can be placed) so JAMES *can find it in this moment. In one quick movement,* JAMES *fastens it to* DONALD.

DONALD *is dragged off, wounded, defeated but roaring insults as he's forced away.* JAMES *turns to* ELLEN.

Am I the champion?

ELLEN (*quiet*). Yes.

JAMES. Am I?

ELLEN *collects herself and pitches it as a shout.*

ELLEN. I declare the champion!

She collects his crown. She takes it to him.

She crowns him.

The crowd goes crazy. He raises her good arm and presents her to the crowd.

JAMES. The Queen of the Fight!

The loudest cheers of all.

Am I your King?

Will you follow me?!

The crowd roars.

Scotland, will you follow me?!

They roar and chant.

JAMES *and* ELLEN *bow. They walk out of the arena.*

Backstage

He's binding up her arm.

JAMES. I *told* you no to dae that!

ELLEN. I'm sorry. But I was right. It made a better show…

JAMES (*cuts her off*). It wasny a show! That's the hale point! Now smile at me like I've jist risked my life for Scotland and won!

She's helping him into his royal robes.

Christ, did it work? They cheered loud enough… did it work?

They walk back into the arena, which is being laid out for a banquet as the crowd still cheers.

JAMES *relaxes, soaking it up.*

We did it, we did it, we did it…

(*To* ELLEN.) *Will you fucking smile?*

She does. They soak up the applause.

Music. JAMES *turns to her.*

Now listen, you need tae find your sense o' humour. You need tae remember this is a royal show and it's about what your King needs, no what you need, no what you want, what the *Crown* needs. That's the nasty fucking job I dae every day and doesny always mak me happy either. So you will smile, you will support me and we will get through this.

ELLEN. What do you mean?

But he's moving into –

Arena/Banquet

JAMES. Where's Peter? What's to happen now? Are we having entertainment or not?

PETER *is there.*

PETER. As soon as you take your place, Your Majesty.

JAMES. Good.

He moves off. ELLEN *goes to follow.*

PETER. No. You'll not sit at the King's table tonight.

ELLEN. What's happening?

PETER. They've changed the script.

ELLEN. Who has?

PETER. I'm sorry, alright? That's your spot there. When you want your exit, just gie me a nod.

ELLEN. What?

But PETER *has gone and* DUNBAR *is there.*

He's taking a moment, getting ready, maybe reading, sorting paper.

DUNBAR. Before I start, let's praise our Queen. Our true Queen. Our real Queen. Beautiful Margaret.

He encourages applause.

(*Pitching over applause.*) Aye! Queen Margaret, the most generous and lovely queen any makar could ever serve, she carries the joy and hope of Scotland within her.

He bows low to MARGARET, *who is soaking up the applause,* DAME PHEMY *beside her.*

But I'm talking of another queen tonight. The Queen of the Fight, is that what we're still calling her? The lovely *Ellen.*

(*To* ELLEN.) Dark lady, this is for you. A good *flyting*…

He starts his poem.

Long have I talked of ladies white,
Noo of a black yin I'll indite,
That landed forth of the last ships,
I'll sketch her likeness, hope it's right,
My lady with the muckle lips.

This starts to get laughs.

So she's all mouth just like an ape,
Or like a puddock with her gape,
And look, her short cat's nose up skips
And see she shines like washing soap
My lady with the muckle lips.

When she's dressed in rich apparel
She shines as bright as a tar barrel.

ELLEN *has been standing, frozen. Now she strides forward and snatches the pages from him.*

A moment.

She starts to read.

ELLEN.

When she was born sun tholed eclipse,
Night loves to fight her every quarrel,
My lady with the muckle lips.

When for her sake with spear and shield,
Men prove they're mightier than their peers,
They kiss and with her get to grips,
And from then on her love is theirs,
My lady with the muckle lips.

But when instead a man is shamed,
Not worthy of the warrior's name,
Her arse before their kiss she slips,
No other comfort can they claim,
From my lady with the muckle lips.

She looks round them all.

Was that enough?

(*To* JAMES.) Was that enough, to please the Crown?

(*To the crowd.*) Was that enough, to *entertain* you? What mair do you want? No, tell me, Scotland, what do you want? I've performed, for you, I sang, for you, I trusted you mair than a bairn trusts its mither's airms, I *bled* for you.

God save me for a *fiel,* I gave you all the love that was in me!

You want mair? You want me cut doon and braken and battered tae mak you mair?

It canny be done.

She's on DUNBAR *now. Unnoticed,* PETER *is readying a trick.*

Nothing will ever mak *you* mair, your soul's just a jealous cur that'll whine and whine behind the likes o' me for a' time. And noo we've a' seen it. We've a' seen that clear.

She looks at PETER, *nods, she wants her exit.*

DUNBAR. Fuck's sake. It was jist a joke…

ELLEN. A joke?

A *joke*?!

She turns back on JAMES.

Scotland, you're the joke.

A moment then BAM! PETER *lets off an explosion or burst of noise.*

Everyone turns.

When they turn back ELLEN *is gone. Confused reactions. Noise and uproar.* PETER *hurries off.* JAMES *is looking for* ELLEN. DAME PHEMY *grabs him and pulls him to* MARGARET, *all very quick and confused, then we see –*

ELLEN, *performing the story of her headlong escape from Edinburgh.*

I ran intae the park, try and stop me, jist *try*! Naebody stopped me there, naebody saw me there. I had the claes on my back and the jewels at my throat and *what need I mair*?!

I was at Dalkeith at dark mirk midnight… A cowman called tae me tae stop, I hissed at him and sent him fleeing.

I was at Pathead an hoor before dawn and my feet were raw and aching all the way up tae the teeth in my heid. But get oot my road, *get oot my road*! I'm walking yet!

The geese hissed at me and I hissed back. Folks banged their doors at the sight of me, the bairns screamed, the milk spilt, a cart drove in a ditch and I turned on the quaking quine that hauled at the horse and I said, *Tak me oot o' here!*

And the road bumped the anger frae me. The cold chilled the fire in me. Oh, Mother of God, I've naething but the claes on my back and the jewels at my throat. Oh save me, whit have I done? I was oot the cart at Ancrum. They were following me by Linton, mair and mair, hunting me like a hare… I lost them by the water lying in the dank dirt like a drookit doe…

I cam minassing tae Minto, a rock in my hand and my teeth ready tae chew them a'. A man stood in my path, they're all aboot me, they're coming at me and then…!

Suddenly ANNE *is there, shouting at* ELLEN*'s pursuers.*

ANNE. Get awa frae her, ye gypet gawpies, on your road!

ELLEN *is telling the story,* ANNE *is still in it.*

ELLEN. There you were.

And you said…

ANNE. We'll beat you! We'll pummel you, we'll smash your heids! Get awa frae my hame!

A moment. ANNE *and* ELLEN *look at each other.*

ELLEN. And hame is any place you and I are together.

And now ANNE *is outside the story too but still in the same place, years later, still with* ELLEN.

Outside Teviot Haugh Castle

ANNE. If that was true you'd stay. And you never do.

ELLEN. I've shows to make, audiences the length o' the land tae dazzle and delight.

And I aye come back.

ANNE. That's the best story you tell.

ELLEN. Because I can tell it wi' you.

ANNE. What show are you takin roond the touns noo? Can you show me a bit o' that?

ELLEN. Aye! Wait till you see…

(*Strikes a pose.*) Lady Anne, we bring you, the sorrowful spectacle of battle lost and worlds ended! But watch and learn how Scotland still survives!

This is the tale of King James. Good King James. *Your* King. One man! One sword! Every man loved him. Every man followed him when battle came at last…

We see JAMES, *he's on high ground rousing his army.*

JAMES. Scotland! Get ready!

ELLEN. The coomen frae Dalkeith, the cottars frae Newbattle. Earl of Cassels, Earl o' Crawford, Earl o' Rothel – they followed him tae Flodden Field.

JAMES *and others are saying their lines over* ELLEN*'s recitation of the dead…*

JAMES. Do you see me?! Get ready tae see me win!

And then we see DUNBAR *beside* JAMES, *staring in horror at the advancing English army.*

DUNBAR. I was a really good makar, I was, I dinnae deserve this. I'm brought tae this for wanting a wage?

JAMES. Scotland! Follow me!

TURNBULL *is there.*

TURNBULL. King James, I'll follow you through the back door of hell!

ELLEN (*under their lines*). The laddies o' Lauder, the toon clerks o' Earlston, Lord Douglas, Lord Cockburn and the bold Lord o' Riccarton. The archers o' Ancrum, the soutars o' Selkirk, Jedburgh, Kelso… Boswells and a'!

JAMES. Follow me!

And JAMES *is gone, running into the dark.*

DUNBAR. Aw Christ, *no*! I'm falling in the dark noo. So may you all!

DUNBAR *is gone. A terrible cacophony of death and destruction.* ELLEN *pitches over it.*

ELLEN. Scotland, your dearest sons are dying in the mud at Flodden! Scotland, your King has fallen and gone!

We see and hear MARGARET. *She is holding a baby. She doubles over screaming in rage and grief.*

MARGARET. *No!!*

The battle is over. The dead lie where they fell. The baby is crying.

ELLEN. But Scotland, you have a king again.

DAME PHEMY *and* PETER *come to* MARGARET. *They take the baby from her as she collapses, weeping.* DAME PHEMY *is close to tears herself. She's addressing a crowd.*

DAME PHEMY. The best of us are deid but we will survive this! Scotland, remember… remember who you are…

She's can't go on. PETER *takes over, lifting the baby, rallying the crowd.*

PETER. Scotland, you still have a king! And we will honour him! We will serve him! King James the Fifth, King of Scots!

He raises the baby. Freezes.

ELLEN. And so we end.

All the 'performers' have drifted away like ghosts. It's just ELLEN *and* ANNE.

ANNE. You still think of him.

ELLEN. Canny not.

ANNE. He must have known where you were. He was King after all and you could never hide. He must have known.

ELLEN. I thought that too, and cursed him but… he got his heir in the end, eh? Poor wee baby King James… I'm glad, now, that he left me tae find my own way. I'm a wild creature o' the woods and hills, nae soul on earth commands my song.

ANNE. Was he a good king?

ELLEN. Nae such thing. The job's too big.

ANNE. Oh are we no wise now. Are we no *wise*?!

They laugh.

I heard a lassie in St Boswell's singing a song o' yours. And my cowman tried tae tell me a joke last month I *knew* was yours. But he messed up the punchline.

ELLEN. Oh aye, the best o' my words and songs will live longer than me, long after my name's deid. Has it been a hard year?

ANNE. Aye, it's been a year, of course it has, a year since Turnbull fell with his King… Times it was hard but… The crop was good, the tups all lambed and all my bairns are living yet with this earth under their feet and my blood pumping roond them. What mair wealth need I?

ELLEN. And whit ither hame will I ever need but here, wi' you, telling the story that's oors alane.

ANNE *starts to sing the song we heard at the beginning, now it has Scots words.*

ANNE.
I heard twa quines at Teviot Haugh
'All that we loued is wede awa.
The flooers o the forest

Smoke and weeds a' the craws left
Oor hame's a hairt that huds jist twa.'

ELLEN *speaks to us – she's between her world and ours, speaking directly to us as if for the first time.*

ELLEN. When oor story's over and done, know this… If our names are forgotten remember we were still real. The songs were sung and heard and all the dances had their steps. The deid were living as you live now.

The poem was real jist as the makar made it.

Remember that maist of all.

ANNE *has finished the song. She opens her arms for the embrace.* ELLEN *steps into her arms and they hold each other.*

Glossary of Scots Words

Gypet gawpies – uncouth folk who are staring
Een – Eyes
Neb – Nose
Lugs – Ears
Mou – Mouth
Oxter – Armpit
Wame – Stomach
Hurdies – Hips
Taes – Toes
Quine – Woman
Chiel – Man
Makar – Poet
Twae – Two
Loon – Boy
The morra – Tomorrow
Drouth – Drought, thirst
Skelp – Slap
Bairn – Child
Wha kens? – Who knows?
Braw – Beautiful
A flyting – A roasting
Sleekit – Weasly, cunning in a pejorative sense
Drookit – Soaking wet
Hairt – Heart
Wede – Withered